NEIL PHILLIPSON is an Associate of Oracy Cambridge and a freelance provider of training and support to schools with a focus on dialogic education. He was a local authority and National Strategies science consultant, and is a long-serving hub-leader with the Primary Science Quality Mark.

RUPERT WEGERIF is Professor of Education at the University of Cambridge, UK. He helped to develop the Thinking Together approach to oracy education that underpins this book, and has spent 30 years researching and writing on the theory and practice of dialogic education.

Thinking Together in Primary Science

Thinking Together in Primary Science offers eight fully resourced lesson plans aimed at ages 9–11 to get teachers and primary-aged children talking together about science and how scientists think and learn as a community. The lessons will help children to form a stronger relationship with science and to understand how scientific thinking can help them in everyday life.

By secondary school, many young people have already decided that science is not for them. One implication of this is that people are less likely to adopt a "scientific mindset" when evaluating the information they encounter online. Understanding the nature of science – what it is and the ways of thinking associated with it – helps young people to identify with the subject and can protect them from everyday misinformation. The book introduces children to key ideas, such as the tentative nature of scientific knowledge, the importance of scepticism, and the role of evidence. It highlights how science can be trusted because of the collaborative way the scientific community generates, tests, and refines knowledge over time.

The book empowers teachers to teach science with greater depth and meaning while embedding oracy into the curriculum. Building on the evidence-based Thinking Together approach, it uses stories to spark dialogue that deepens children's understanding of science, fosters a closer connection to the subject, and helps protect them from the misinformation so prevalent in today's world.

"*Thinking Together in Primary Science* explains, in a clear and accessible way, why it is important that scientific thinking comes alive for young people through dialogue and discussion. But this book does much more: it provides teachers with practical guidance and resources, developed from classroom-based research, to make this happen successfully in their classrooms."

Neil Mercer, *Emeritus Professor of Education, Hughes Hall, University of Cambridge, UK*

"This practical, research-informed guide to 'thinking together' offers clear ground rules and engaging talk activities that help pupils develop the habits of mind underpinning scientific thinking. Using the UKS2 science curriculum as a rich context, it is a valuable resource for Year 5 and 6 teachers developing oracy."

Jane Turner, *University of Hertfordshire (former Director, Primary Science Quality Mark), UK*

"This book provides practical guidance for educators seeking to promote collaboration and curiosity in primary science. This timely publication offers a pedagogy that will enable children to understand that the question of '...how do you know?' helps to navigate both the challenges of science and their social media-fuelled lives."

Natasha Serret, *Associate Professor of Science Education, Nottingham Trent University, UK*

Neil Phillipson and Rupert Wegerif

Thinking Together in Primary Science

An Oracy-Based Approach to Teaching About the Nature of Science and Scientific Thinking

Routledge
Taylor & Francis Group
LONDON AND NEW YORK

TTiPS

Designed cover image: Getty Images

First published 2027
by Routledge
4 Park Square, Milton Park, Abingdon, Oxon OX14 4RN

and by Routledge
605 Third Avenue, New York, NY 10158

Routledge is an imprint of the Taylor & Francis Group, an informa business

© 2027 Neil Phillipson and Rupert Wegerif

The right of Neil Phillipson and Rupert Wegerif to be identified as authors of this work has been asserted in accordance with sections 77 and 78 of the Copyright, Designs and Patents Act 1988.

All rights reserved. No part of this book may be reprinted or reproduced or utilised in any form or by any electronic, mechanical, or other means, now known or hereafter invented, including photocopying and recording, or in any information storage or retrieval system, without permission in writing from the publishers.

For Product Safety Concerns and Information please contact our EU representative GPSR@taylorandfrancis.com. Taylor & Francis Verlag GmbH, Kaufingerstraße 24, 80331 München, Germany.

Trademark notice: Product or corporate names may be trademarks or registered trademarks, and are used only for identification and explanation without intent to infringe.

British Library Cataloguing-in-Publication Data
A catalogue record for this book is available from the British Library

ISBN: 978-1-041-12177-0 (hbk)
ISBN: 978-1-041-12173-2 (pbk)
ISBN: 978-1-003-66345-4 (ebk)

DOI: 10.4324/9781003663454

Typeset in Bembo
by SPi Technologies India Pvt Ltd (Straive)

Access the Support Material at www.routledge.com/9781041121732

In the hope of a more dialogic world.

Contents

Supporting resources

Each lesson in the book has an associated PowerPoint presentation. These presentations include slides to support each stage of the lesson: the warm-up activity, the story stimulus and associated discussion plan, the main activity, and the plenary.

For some lessons, a printable pupil worksheet is available.

Readers can access these resources at www.routledge.com/9781041121732.

Acknowledgements

This work would not have been possible without the support of Dr Ron Zimmern, Fellow of Hughes Hall, Cambridge.

The book grew out of the work of Dr Laura Kerslake. Supported by Judith Hannam and Rupert Wegerif at Hughes Hall, Cambridge, Laura developed an original series of lesson plans as part of the Inquiring Science project. A number of the stories and exercises she created have been adapted for inclusion in the book. We are grateful to Laura for this work and for her ongoing support.

We are also grateful to Shenpeng Shi for his support with the organisation of the project.

The lesson plans included in the book were trialled by teachers and children in schools in Stoke-on-Trent and Cheshire. We are particularly grateful to David Badley, then of St Peter's C of E Primary School in Newton-le-Willows, Dawn McCann of Hillside Primary School in Stoke-on-Trent, and Sinead Carroll-Knight of Our Lady and St Benedict Catholic Academy in Stoke-on-Trent for their support and their invaluable feedback.

We continued to consult with David Badley, now of Beamont Primary Academy in Warrington, throughout the manuscript preparation process and are very grateful for his enthusiasm, experience, and insight.

We are very aware of the need for oracy-based approaches to teaching and learning to be inclusive of all pupils, and we are grateful to Wendy Lee of Lingo for her contribution to the book.

Introduction

This book — *Thinking Together in Primary Science*, or **TTiPS** – is a practical classroom guide written with two aims in mind.

First, it enables you to teach children about the **nature of science** – what it is, the ways of thinking associated with it, and how these ways of thinking can help us in everyday life.

Second, it will help you embed **evidence-based oracy approaches** in the curriculum. In particular, it will help you develop effective classroom dialogue or *Thinking Together*.

There's an important connection between these aims. We believe that a dialogic approach enables children to make sense of potentially abstract ideas about science and scientific thinking and to connect them to their own experiences, making the learning more meaningful.

Let's begin, though, by asking ourselves why young children should take the trouble to learn about the nature of science at all.

DOI: 10.4324/9781003663454-1

Why is "the nature of science" worth learning about?

In a 2023 report, the Primary Curriculum Advisory Group (PCAG) in the UK proposed a framework for the planning of a future primary science curriculum.[1] They emphasised the importance of giving all children opportunities to relate new learning to personal experience and to develop an *identity* with science.

This theme of identity is echoed in a 2023 survey commissioned by the Royal Society and EngineeringUK, which includes a measure of "science identity" – the extent to which secondary school students in the UK might be considered to have a relationship with science.[2] Only 9 per cent were classified as having a strong science identity, while a third (32 per cent) felt that science was "not for me."

This lack of identity with science contributes to young people's diminishing interest in and enjoyment of the subject as they move through school.[3] This has obvious societal and economic implications, and it may also leave young people less willing and able to adopt a "scientific mindset" in everyday life. This matters because there's evidence to suggest that scientific ways of thinking could help young people to more safely navigate the abundance of information to which they're exposed, particularly online.[4]

The urgency of this issue is underlined by the final report of England's Curriculum and Assessment Review, which emphasises strongly the need for improved media literacy so that young people are protected from misinformation. The review states that science supports the development of the critical analysis which underpins media literacy and includes the lines:

> …our engagement has underscored the importance of ensuring that the Science curriculum supports young people to deal with misinformation and other challenges. It is vital that the Science curriculum equips children and young people, across all key stages, with the skills to evaluate scientific claims critically, assess evidence from multiple sources and understand how science operates in everyday life.[5]

So how can we encourage more young people to develop a personal relationship with science? The PCAG report emphasises the value of giving children the knowledge and agency to be responsible global citizens. It highlights the importance of providing children with experiences that are meaningful, emotionally charged, and imaginatively engaging, and have relevance now, not merely in the future. It also suggests that young people are more likely to identify with science if they develop an understanding of its nature and practices.

The report proposes the following learning descriptors to guide future curriculum planning:

- **Science is a creative human endeavour** which builds new knowledge to explain natural phenomena.
- **Science is an empirically based process** derived from observation of the natural world.
- **Scientific knowledge is tentative** and subject to change based on new evidence or new interpretations of existing evidence.
- **Science is a rigorous discipline** where it is important to know how the evidence was collected and whether it can be trusted.

The TTiPS lessons address all these points.

To identify with science, young people need an appreciation of how this creative human endeavour works. It may be helpful for them to understand science as a *community of practice*. Science can be perceived as being advanced by isolated individuals — perhaps eccentric geniuses speaking a language that most of us can't understand. This can make science seem detached from the world, inaccessible, and unattractive. It also raises questions about the extent to which we can trust or relate to the knowledge generated in this way. After all, these isolated scientists are surely subject to human frailties including bias and zealotry (Frankenstein certainly had a few faults!).

In reality, most modern scientists are part of an interactive global community. They share standards of practice, and they openly share their research so that it can be rigorously reviewed and built upon by their peers. They correct each other's errors, including those caused by bias, which means that the community as a whole shows humility: it remains open to correction and further learning.

Scientists are, in fact, part of an ongoing **dialogue** in which knowledge is created, tested, and revised; the dialogue extends back into the past and forward into the future, and it's a dialogue that our young people can aspire to contribute to. That seems to be an important message if we want science to be a subject that they identify with.

In a small way, by learning to engage in better dialogue — to *think together* — about science in the TTiPS lessons, children are getting a taste of what it is to be a part of that wider cultural conversation. Yet to understand how the scientific community works, they must also develop conceptual understanding of evidence, argumentation, and reasoning.

Primary teachers in the UK are already familiar with the concept of disciplinary knowledge and are used to teaching the practical skills needed to work scientifically. They may be less familiar, and perhaps less confident, with the idea of teaching pupils about the reasoning processes through which scientific knowledge is generated, tested, and revised.

TTiPS will support you in helping children develop this kind of understanding in a relatable, meaningful way so that they begin to form a strong and lasting relationship with the subject — one that will benefit them in their everyday lives, now and in the future.

Why adopt an oracy-based approach?

In its 2024 report, "We need to talk," the UK's Oracy Education Commission defined oracy as:

> Articulating ideas, developing understanding and engaging with others through speaking, listening and communication.[6]

The Commission made a strong case for prioritising oracy in education, arguing that it's intrinsic to children's early development, the testing of thought, social and emotional well-being, confidence, and the ability to challenge and debate issues constructively. They recommended recognising oracy as the fourth "R" (alongside reading, writing, and arithmetic) and that it should be seen as an entitlement of every child's education.

This recommendation is reflected in the guidance provided by Ofsted, England's education regulator, for school inspectors in 2025. The guidance places oracy alongside reading, writing, and mathematics as essential for accessing the wider curriculum. Inspectors are directed to consider whether:

> All pupils are explicitly taught how to communicate effectively through spoken language (oracy), articulate ideas, develop understanding and engage with others through speaking, listening and communication.[7]

At the time of writing, the UK government has undertaken to develop a framework to support oracy practice in English schools to complement existing frameworks for reading and writing.

It seems inevitable, then, that more schools in England will look to "teach oracy." We very much welcome this — there's a wealth of evidence to suggest that the ability to use speaking, listening, and nonverbal communication for a variety of purposes enhances young people's cognitive, personal, and social development. It improves their ability to learn and increases the likelihood that they will find their learning meaningful and enjoyable.

However, teachers will need guidance on what teaching oracy effectively actually involves. In his 2025 book, *Oracy: The Transformative Power of Finding Your Voice*, Professor Neil Mercer identifies three interdependent aspects of oracy:

- **Learning how to talk**. Developing students' spoken language skills
- **Learning through talk**. Using talk effectively for teaching and learning

- **Learning about talk**. Understanding the nature of spoken language and how it works[8]

Organisations such as Oracy Cambridge and Voice 21 provide advice, resources, and training to support teachers in addressing these aspects.[9]

Mercer proposes that learning about talk belongs primarily in the English curriculum, learning through talk should be embedded across subjects, and learning how to talk may be taught either in dedicated oracy lessons or woven through day-to-day teaching.

TTiPS covers all three aspects while maintaining a focus on creating opportunities for children to learn about the nature of science through talk. We hope that you'll find it a useful model for embedding high-quality, evidence-informed oracy practice across the curriculum.

A word on dialogue

Oracy is broad in scope: it includes all the ways in which we use speaking, listening, and nonverbal communication for different purposes. When we think of these different purposes, presentation, debate and collaboration often come to mind, and these are all important uses of language. In Chapter 1, we explore these modes of communication in more detail and refer to them as "talk games."

This book foregrounds one game in particular: collaboration through classroom dialogue. Dialogue is easily overlooked as a mode of communication. It's one of those words that carries different meanings. In an everyday sense, it's often taken to mean any kind of spoken interaction between two or more people. But it can also mean something more specific – something quite special.

The Greek roots of the term are *dia*, which can be translated as "through" or "across," and *logos*, often translated as "the word," "speech," or "reason." This derivation conjures up a number of images or accounts of dialogue. For example, it might be taken to mean speaking or reasoning across difference — the different perspectives and understandings that often divide us.

The American physicist and dialogue expert David Bohm explained it like this:

> When one person says something, the other person does not in general respond with exactly the same meaning as that seen by the first person.... Thus, when the second person replies, the first person sees a difference between what he meant to say and what has been understood.... He may then be able to see something new which is relevant both to his own views and to those of the other person.[10]

Dialogue, in this sense, is a creative act — it generates new meaning that can be held in common between the participants. For Bohm, such shared meaning is the glue that holds people — and societies — together.

The ability to reason across difference and to generate shared understanding is profoundly important. Sadly, a glance at world events shows how rare and difficult it can be. Teaching children to engage in dialogue well is therefore a gift of hope for a future in which all our voices are heard with respect and contribute to a shared understanding of our human experience. A good oracy education must involve teaching *for* dialogue as a valuable outcome in its own right, as well as teaching *through* dialogue as a powerful means of deepening understanding of the curriculum.

To help us understand how it enables deeper understanding of subjects, let's look back at Bohm's account. What if the first speaker were a teacher and the second a pupil? When the pupil responds, the teacher — if she is disposed to truly listen — may hear a difference between what she meant to say and what has been understood, and this becomes an opportunity.

If the teacher — and, perhaps, the pupil — can inhabit both perspectives for a while, they may be able to see something new. This may be something that illuminates their subject further, or it may be a greater awareness of their different ways of seeing. The crucial thing is that more than one perspective is valued and each person's horizon is expanded. This is what it means to teach — and learn — *through* dialogue.

We have explored ideas about dialogue in education — and argued for its importance — in more detail elsewhere.[11]

Thinking together

There are different views on what counts as dialogue in the classroom. Some argue that true dialogue is difficult when one person — most obviously the teacher — holds more authority than others, or when a group is trying to converge on a single "right answer" or a shared decision. We needn't be too concerned about that here. Throughout this book, we use the term **thinking together** to mean any interaction in which two or more perspectives are heard, valued, and used to create better understanding. Interactions that involve this inter-animation of different voices can be said to be "dialogic," even if some would not call them "true dialogue."

The term "thinking together" is closely associated with the pedagogical approach developed by Neil Mercer, Rupert Wegerif, and Lyn Dawes in the 1990s.[12] While observing pupils collaborating in small groups, they noticed that successful groups seemed to hold some shared beliefs about how they should behave. Helping the pupils reflect on these beliefs and make them explicit enabled the co-creation of ground rules for talk. Regular use of these ground rules significantly improved the quality of group discussion.

This points to an important conclusion: **effective collaborative group work is far more likely if children are taught how to do it**. Anyone who has observed children working in groups will have noticed that it doesn't always go well! This leads some people to claim that group work is ineffective, despite evidence to the contrary.[13] Neil Mercer argues that we shouldn't be surprised by the challenges children face:

> Students are being expected to carry on a reasoned discussion, but they may rarely encounter such dialogue in their lives. Why should they be expected to know how to do it in school? They need to be taught how to work in groups.[14]

The creation and consistent use of a set of ground rules is a tried and tested method for teaching effective thinking together, and it's the approach promoted in this book. You can read more about the Thinking Together approach and find practical advice on the development and use of ground rules in Chapter 2 and in Appendix 1.

From teacher to facilitator – and back again

Ground rules are a useful tool for improving the quality of pupil–pupil interactions as they collaborate in small groups. The behaviours they describe, though, are equally useful when the whole class is thinking together. One significant difference in whole-class talk is the participation of the teacher.

In Chapter 1, we liken different modes of communication to different "talk games." This analogy can be extended to describe the different games teachers play with language. Sometimes we give presentations (or monologues) — when giving explanations or instructions, for example. No interaction is needed, and the rules of the game as far as the pupils are concerned revolve around listening carefully.

Sometimes we do interact with the pupils, but without a real interest in what they are thinking — perhaps to elicit the "right answer" for everyone to hear once more. This game often involves questions requiring a short answer, which the teacher can evaluate; the trick for the pupil is to give the teacher the answer she is looking for.[15]

In both cases, the teacher can be said to be in an **authoritative** mode. The aim of the game is to transmit or reinforce information. This is not bad teaching! It's essential. But we must heed Bohm's warning: "When one person says something, the other person does not in general respond with exactly the same meaning as that seen by the first person…." The sense that children make of the information we transmit is probably not quite the sense we intended!

There are times, then, when a teacher needs to step back from transmission and focus on listening so that he can "see a difference between what he meant to say and what has been understood." The task is to create a shared understanding by holding the pupils' perspectives together with his own and creating space for these different points of view to "play with each other."

If there is a single right answer to be understood, the job is to help the pupils make the creative leap from their own understandings to the one held by the teacher — or to something closer to it. This is a process in which the pupils must be active. They must reconstruct their understandings by reflecting, noticing how their position differs from others, testing the explanatory power of their ideas, adapting them, and so on.

In other cases, such as sharing interpretations of a poem, there is no single right answer. Here, the teacher's job is to help everyone share, hear the different perspectives, and, hopefully, create a richer shared appreciation of the subject in hand.

In either situation, the teacher is required to play a different game, shifting from the authoritative mode of transmission to the dialogic mode of facilitation. The aim is to get everyone thinking together. This isn't as easy as it sounds — like all good games, it requires practice. Here's some advice that may help you develop your skills:

1 **Get ready to listen**. Teaching through dialogue is more about attitude than technique. It involves turning to your students with genuine interest in and openness towards what they have to say — and in a class full of children it's not easy! Practise quietening your mind — not thinking about what you might say next (the opposite of listening is preparing to speak!), not rushing to judgement, not thinking about an impending break duty — just listening and seeking to understand. It's important to model this kind of listening so that pupils come to understand that everyone should be listened to, and that their voices are an essential and valued component of the process of teaching and learning.
2 **Suspend judgement**. Resist the temptation to evaluate a pupil's initial response: "Yes, that's right," or "No, I don't think you have quite understood." Give yourself time to process what's been said before deciding how to respond. You have a range of "talk moves" such as those listed below to choose from, or you may decide to remain silent to create the space for others to respond — you don't need to speak every second turn!

3 **Help pupils to be heard and understood**.[16] I attended an international conference recently, organised by the Academy of Professional Dialogue. We talked about the barriers to creating "dialogic classrooms." A teacher from Buenos Aires spoke of a culture of fear of getting the wrong answer or asking a question that shows you are struggling to understand — a fear that seems pervasive in her school. People from the UK, South Africa, Iran, the USA, and other countries reported similar experiences.

So, an important early step is to create a safe and positive environment for thinking together. We need to give pupils the confidence to share their **authentic voices** and to secure high levels of participation. It's important to let them know that you value what they have to say, not because you want the "correct answer," but because you need to know what sense they have made of what you have tried to teach them: you need to hear their "real" response, not their "let's try to please the teacher" response. Try telling them this, stressing that teaching and learning is a two-way, dialogic process in which they are valued partners. It's important to encourage them to elaborate so they can be properly understood and can develop their ideas.

Relevant talk moves

"Say more."; "Can you give us an example of that?"; "Let me see if I have understood. Are you saying…?"; "Who else has an idea to share?"; give adequate thinking time; make use of partner talk or think, pair, share to reduce threat and encourage more elaborated answers and wider participation.

4 **Encourage pupils to listen to each other**. Just as you need the intention to listen to the pupils, so they need the intention to listen to you and to each other. Just as you need to see them as valued partners in the teaching and learning process, so they need to see each other as valued partners, each with something meaningful to contribute. Each person in the class has a part to play in creating a safe and positive environment, and learning to listen with care and **respect** is essential. This means pupils listening to understand each other, not rushing to make a judgement about whether they agree or disagree. It may involve actively encouraging their peers to elaborate so they can be better understood.

Relevant "talk moves"

"Can anyone put what A said into their own words?"; "Could someone summarise what has been said so far?"; "Is there a question that we need to ask A?"; "What are your take-aways from our talk — what was said that was particularly valuable?"; "Who would you like to thank for their contributions to this talk?"

5 **Encourage pupils to think a little harder**. As a positive environment builds, you can increase the challenge. Tell pupils what you're doing and why. Share with them the questions you'll be looking to ask that call on them to make moves such as giving reasons, looking for alternatives, making connections, and making distinctions. These are the cognitive tools that pupils need if they are to re-construct their understandings and expand their horizons.

Perhaps this is the place to note that, even in a facilitative mode, your **subject knowledge** is crucial, as is the developing subject knowledge of the pupils. The following talk moves are generic, but they will usually be used in the context of a subject area — in this case science. You might be calling for the distinction between a prediction and a hypothesis, or for more precise language to describe the effect of copper "letting heat through it." It's not possible to make the cognitive moves outlined earlier — or to call for them to be made — without relevant subject knowledge.

Relevant "talk moves"

"Why do you think that?"; "What's the evidence for that?"; "How did you reach that conclusion?"; "Is that always true? What if…?"; "Is there a counter-example?"; "What might someone who disagreed say?"; "Are you saying the same thing as A, or something different?"; "How are these things connected?"; "How are these things different?"

6 **Encourage the pupils to think together**. One aim of your facilitation is to make yourself increasingly redundant! As time goes on, you should need to make fewer interventions in the group's dialogue because pupils will be more accustomed to giving reasons, considering alternatives, and so on. If these moves are being made, you don't need to call for them. If they're not being made, perhaps you can encourage the pupils to call for them.

Your role is to ensure that the pupils keep on thinking well and thinking together. There's an important difference between a series of contributions from different pupils that are unrelated (a series of monologues, if you will) and a continuous chain of shared thinking (a dialogue). You need to get the pupils responding to, building on, and questioning each other's thoughts. Your silence can be powerful here because it creates the space and time for them to think and respond, and it implicitly creates the expectation that they do it.

Relevant "talk moves"

"What do people think about what A said?"; "Who agrees / disagrees"; "Who would like to respond to A?"; "Can we take this idea further?"; "Can we build on that?"; "Is there a different point of view / are there other possibilities?"; "A, could you ask B to say more / give a reason / if there is evidence for that," etc.

7 **Be prepared to return to the authoritative mode**. I once watched a class thinking together about how we see the moon. The teacher was hoping that the pupils would apply their learning about light sources and reflection to explain that we see the moon because light from the sun reflects from it and into our eyes. Unexpectedly, an alternative explanation was offered: we see the moon because the sun goes behind it and shines through it!

The teacher chose to stay in dialogic mode for a while, testing and encouraging others to test the new idea. Ultimately, though, the teacher is accountable to accurate subject knowledge: it's not legitimate to end this episode of thinking together by saying, "Great – so we have two different explanations of how we see the moon. Choose the one that makes most sense to you."

In the end, the teacher must resume authority, reinforcing and perhaps re-explaining the accepted answer. In a sense the teacher remains dialogic – the new explanation is addressed to the children with their alternative ideas in mind, but they must also be clear that the alternative explanation is incorrect.

The ability to switch between different modes of communication — different talk games — and to match them to the desired learning outcome is important, and is a matter of developing pedagogical judgement, supported by sound subject knowledge.

From thinking in general to thinking like scientists

Science as we now think of it emerged in the mid-seventeenth century, out of lively networks of correspondence and inquiry among European thinkers. *The Journal des sçavans* (Paris, January 1665) and the *Philosophical Transactions of the Royal Society* (London, March 1665) are two of the earliest periodicals that helped shape this new public conversation about understanding the world.

Over time, this open conversation became more specialised. Different kinds of inquiry gradually formed their own disciplines, each with its own standards and focus. Natural science is just one of those strands — in a sense, a *subset* of good thinking in general. What distinguishes it is its particular *emphasis on the careful use of publicly testable evidence to support causal explanations of events.*

Other areas, like history, follow different but equally valid criteria, using evidence to support interpretations of unique events rather than explanations of repeatable events. But behind all the strands of shared inquiry lies the same root: good thinking as a form of open dialogue — paying careful attention, responding thoughtfully, and allowing understanding to develop within a shared space of inquiry.

We hope, then, that learning to think well together in a general sense while exploring the ways of thinking that characterise science will prove a good initiation to scientific discourse. Thinking together provides the habits of mind — attentiveness, responsiveness, openness to alternative ideas — that make scientific thinking possible.

How to use this book

Fitting it into the curriculum

The TTiPS lessons are designed for teaching as part of the upper Key Stage Two science curriculum in England — that is for pupils from nine to eleven years old.

The first two lessons serve as an introduction to Thinking Together and we hope that teachers will find them useful in supporting learning across the curriculum. It may be that they are best used at the beginning of the school year.

We recommend that the science-focused lessons are used in the order provided. Colleagues who trialled the lessons felt that they would like to teach them as a sequence early in the year because they enable classes to examine the Key Stage Two topics through the lens of evidence and the various forms of thinking introduced. It may be, though, that some teachers prefer to spread the lessons over the course of a year, perhaps teaching one during each half-term.

Colleagues also noted overlap between the TTiPS lessons, personal, social, health, and economic education (PSHE), and citizenship education. These connections arise because of the emphasis TTiPS places on teaching *for* dialogue and on protection from misinformation and fake news. It may be, then, that some curriculum time allocated to PSHE or citizenship can be used for TTiPS.

In Chapter 9, we provide an example of how the TTiPS approach could act as a frame for a sequence of teaching episodes on the theme of dissolving.

Introduction to the TTiPS lessons

This book contains eight chapters that include a fully resourced lesson plan. The first two chapters are focused on oracy education and the remaining six are focused on the nature of science.

Lesson 1 sets the scene by introducing pupils to the different ways in which we use language to achieve different goals: they are introduced to the idea of "talk games." Lesson 2 focuses on the game of Thinking Together and enables the class to co-construct a set of ground-rules that will guide them to play the game well.

For the remainder of the lessons, pupils explore different aspects of the nature of science and the ways of thinking that shape it. Ideas about empiricism, reasoning, evidence and the scientific community are introduced in a way that supports pupils to make sense of them by connecting them to their own experiences.

Each chapter begins with a section of "Notes for the Curious Teacher". These are for teachers with the interest — and time — to dig just a little deeper into the ideas underpinning the associated lesson. They come with questions to support your own critical reflection. You shouldn't view these as required reading; each lesson plan begins with a short section of "Notes for the Busy Teacher" which provide a concise summary of essential background knowledge for those short of time.

Lesson structure

Each of the lessons follows a common structure.

Warm-up

The primary aim of the warm-up exercise is to foreground one ground rule or skill involved in thinking together and to allow the pupils to practise its application.

During Lesson 2, you and your class will explore the skills and behaviours that enable effective group work and produce a set of ground rules to guide you. Your ground rules may well recognise the importance of skills and behaviours such as listening, including everyone's views, and challenging ideas respectfully.

However, enacting these things isn't as easy as it might sound. In what different ways can we respond to each other, and what language do we need? What does challenging others respectfully actually look and sound like? These are skills that need deliberate teaching and deliberate practice, and the warm-up exercises provide opportunities for just that.

Stimulus

The stimulus takes the form of a story featuring the pupils and teachers of a fictional school, Newton Primary. These pupils are usually grappling with an issue related to an aspect of scientific thinking, but in the context of their own lives. The story, therefore, serves as a bridge between potentially abstract ideas (like inductive reasoning) and the children's world.

The story can be read by the teacher, or displayed for pupils to share the reading, perhaps a sentence or two at a time. This is a useful opportunity for oracy education: it provides pupils with the opportunity to speak in front of the class and — if met with respectful listening — helps to build a climate in which it feels safe to take such a risk.

That feeling of safety can be lost if pupils feel pushed to read, so it's advisable to give everyone the right to say "pass" if they don't feel comfortable. Be patient in your attempts to build a highly participatory classroom environment — if you build the safe space, provide the necessary support, and if the lesson content is appropriately engaging, more and more pupils will feel the "pull" to collaborate.

Discussion plan

Each stimulus is followed by a series of questions or "discussion plan" intended to help you draw children's attention to significant points in the story and to help them to begin to understand how the story is connected to science. The questions tend to move from being specific to the story (concrete) to being about more general ideas (abstract).

You should not feel that you have to use each question in turn! The plans are for guidance only and should be used flexibly. They are there to help you to **facilitate** the pupils' thinking, enabling them to make the cognitive and social moves that are characteristic of good thinking together and to make meaning of the story and the ideas embedded in it.

The stories are designed to stimulate children's curiosity so it may be a good idea to spend a little time gathering any comments or questions they have. You could invite them to reflect on and share anything they find puzzling or interesting in the story. Any questions that emerge could be addressed immediately or collected and referred to as the session goes on. This would be a good way of encouraging a sense of shared inquiry.

Exercise

Having used the stimulus and discussion plan to introduce the lesson content in a relatable way, the main exercise in each lesson moves the pupils into an exploration of how the relevant behaviours and ways of thinking are used in science. After initial modelling by the teacher, the exercises provide opportunities for small group work and thinking together.

Plenary

Each exercise concludes with a whole-class plenary which attempts to draw the threads of the lesson together and revisit the problems raised in the stimulus.

Metacognition

The final part of the lesson is an opportunity to reflect on the pupils' use of the ground rules and their impact. This is important, because it helps pupils to become more aware of how the skills and behaviours they are practising contribute to good thinking together. The hope is that they will then be more likely to apply these skills across the curriculum and in wider contexts: a little prompting from their teachers would certainly help!

Chapter 9 provides an opportunity for you to reflect on what you have taken from the book. You might not want to wait until you have worked through all the lessons before engaging in some of this reflection – we recommend regular visits to this final chapter.

We very much hope that you and your pupils enjoy the TTiPS lessons and that you enjoy thinking together!

Notes

1 Jane Turner, Lynne Bianchi, Ali Eley, Liz Lawrence, and Alex Sinclair. *Primary Curriculum Advisory Group: Framework for a Primary Science Curriculum* (Institute of Physics Publishing Ltd, 2023). Accessed November 2025. https://www.rsb.org.uk/images/edpol/Primary_Curriculum_Advisory_Group_report.pdf

2 EngineeringUK and The Royal Society. *Science Education Tracker 2023* (EngineeringUK and The Royal Society, 2024). Accessed November 2025. https://royalsociety.org/-/media/policy/projects/science-education-tracker/science-education-tracker-2023.pdf

3 This trend is well-documented internationally. This interesting report from Canada makes a distinction between interest in science "in-school" and "out-of-school": Patrice Potvin and Abdelkrim Hasni. "Analysis of the Decline in Interest Towards School Science and Technology from Grades 5 Through 11," *Journal of Science Education and Technology* 23, no. 6 (2014): 784–802. https://doi.org/10.1007/s10956-014-9512-x

4 Examples of relevant evidence include: Geneviève Allaire-Duquette, Abdelkrim Hasni, Josianne N. Drouin, Anick Groleau, Ahmed Mahhou, Alexandre Legault, Antoine Khayat, Marie-Ève Carignan, and Jean Philippe Ayotte-Beaudet. "'Primary School Pupils' Ability to Detect Fake Science News Following a News Media Literacy Intervention: Exploration of Their Success Rate, Evaluation Strategies, Self-Efficacy Beliefs, and Views of Science News," *Journal of Digital Educational Technology* 5, no. 2 (2025): ep2509. https://doi.org/10.30935/jdet/15963; Andrea Siani, Mansi Joseph, and Cristina

Dacin. "Susceptibility to Scientific Misinformation and Perception of News Source Reliability in Secondary School Students." *Discover Education* 3 (2024): Article 93. https://doi.org/10.1007/s44217-024-00194-8; Ansley T. Tullos and Jacqueline D. Woolley "The development of children's ability to use evidence to infer reality status." *Child Development* 80, no. 1 (2009): 101–114. https://doi.org/10.1111/j.1467-8624.2008.01248.x; T. K. Hermansen, K. F. Mathisen, and S. Ronfard. "When Children Can Explain Why They Believe a Claim, They Suggest a Better Empirical Test for That Claim." *Royal Society Open Science* 11, no. 12 (2024): 241875. https://doi.org/10.1098/rsos.241875

5 Becky Francis, ed. *Curriculum and Assessment Review Final Report: Building a World-Class Curriculum for All* (Department for Education, 2025), 115. Accessed November 2025. https://assets.publishing.service.gov.uk/media/690b96bbc22e4ed8b051854d/Curriculum_and_Assessment_Review_final_report_-_Building_a_world-class_curriculum_for_all.pdf

6 Oracy Education Commission. *We Need to Talk: The Report of the Commission on the Future of Oracy Education in England* (Voice 21 and Impetus, 2024), 14. Accessed November 2025. https://oracyeducationcommission.co.uk/wp-content/uploads/2024/10/We-need-to-talk-2024.pdf

7 Ofsted. *State-Funded Schools Inspection Toolkit: For Use from November 2025* (Department for Education, 9 September 2025), 19. Accessed November 2025. https://assets.publishing.service.gov.uk/media/68b9a6b8b0a373a01819fe4b/Schools_inspection_toolkit.pdf

8 Neil Mercer. *Oracy: The Transformative Power of Finding Your Voice* (The Bodley Head, 2025).

9 Oracy Cambridge. "Welcome – Oracy Cambridge." Accessed November 2025. https://oracycambridge.org/; Voice 21. "Voice 21 | Oracy | United Kingdom." Accessed November 2025. https://voice21.org/?gad_source=1andgad_campaignid=16884202503andgbraid=0AAAAACn8iZA6g6z4JMKubr4N2_23vJhtYandgclid=CjwKCAiAlMHIBhAcEiwAZhZBUpApffATzhjOLvkslyAbilAGqDQcUhKN6X_4ViuK0MJJ1VUewoLQ2xoCptgQAvD_BwE

10 David Bohm and Lee Nichol, eds. *On Dialogue* (Routledge, 1996), 3.

11 See, for example: Rupert Wegerif. *Rethinking Educational Theory: Education as Expanding Dialogue* (Edward Elgar Publishing, 2025); Neil Phillipson and Rupert Wegerif. *Dialogic Education: Mastering Core Concepts through Thinking Together* (Routledge, 2017); Rupert Wegerif. *Dialogic: Education for the Internet Age* (Routledge, 2012).
12 University of Cambridge. "Thinking Together Project." Accessed November 2025. https://thinkingtogether.educ.cam.ac.uk/
13 Christine Howe. *Peer Groups and Children's Development* (Blackwell, 2010).
14 Neil Mercer. *Oracy: The Transformative Power of Finding Your Voice* (The Bodley Head, 2025), 123.
15 This kind of teacher-pupil interaction is often described as Initiation-Response-Evaluation or IRE. The teacher initiates, often with a closed question requiring a short response. A pupil provides that response, and the teacher quickly evaluates it: "That's right – well done."
16 The framework of "talk moves" suggested here is based on a 2012 document by Sarah Michaels and Cathy O'Connor: The Talk Science Primer. You can read it here: https://inquiryproject.terc.edu/shared/pd/TalkScience_Primer.pdf

1

The games we play

Notes for the curious teacher

In classrooms and in life more generally we use talk in different ways depending on the situation. Sometimes we stand at the front and give a presentation explaining something clearly. Sometimes, we just chat in a light-hearted way to be friendly and share stories. Each way of talking can be thought of as a kind of game with its own aims, moves, rules, and skills.

Wittgenstein and language games

The idea of talk as a kind of game is not new. The philosopher, Ludwig Wittgenstein, suggested that language has a variety of

DOI: 10.4324/9781003663454-2

overlapping uses like a family of related games.[1] He used simple examples of language games – giving orders, reporting an event, telling a joke – to show how language always works in a context: even these everyday uses of language involve shared rules and expectations. Wittgenstein pointed out that the meaning of words is not fixed but comes from how we use them together in real situations.

Bakhtin and speech genres

The Russian thinker, Mikhail Bakhtin, had a similar view. He pointed out that language isn't just about getting words right, it's about using words to do things with other people. He introduced the idea of "speech genres" to describe familiar types of talk used in different situations: chatting with friends, telling a story, giving a scientific explanation. These genres shape what we say, how we say it, and what kind of reply we expect.[2]

As children, we first learn to copy how others speak in different genres. But over time, we learn to make these ways of speaking our own – finding our voice and forming our identity through talk. When pupils are unfamiliar with certain speech genres – like scientific explanation or formal debate – they can struggle to join in. Making these genres visible, inviting, and accessible helps all learners take part.

Why "games"?

Wittgenstein and Bakhtin both help us see language as a series of purposeful social activities. Just as football, chess and hide-and-seek are different games with different rules, so too are the ways we use language to explain, question, joke, persuade, or reflect. Each form of talk is shaped by the expectations of the people playing it. And each has rules that can be learned.

Talk games in school

Our idea of talk games, then, combines ideas from Wittgenstein's language games and Bakhtin's speech genres. The intention is to suggest that pupils need to become familiar with the purposes, rules, and moves of the different communicative games we ask them to play so that they can recognise them and switch between them ("Ah! Now this is chess, not draughts – different game, different rules, different moves!").

With time and practice, they can move from copying the rules to adapting and internalising them. Eventually, they develop confidence to speak in their own voice: "Now this is a game for me. I know how to play."

This book is concerned mainly with the game of classroom dialogue or thinking together, but other games such as presentation, storytelling, and debate can and perhaps should be taught in schools.[3] They help children to join in the many communities they are part of, and they support learning across the curriculum. Teachers might find the Oracy Skills Framework, developed by Oracy Cambridge and Voice 21, to be a useful resource when teaching diverse modes of communication.[4]

As children become fluent in these general-purpose games, they are better prepared for more specialised and complex practices – like scientific discourse – where the rules are reshaped by the purposes and ways of thinking of different disciplines. So, learning to think together in a way that is generally applicable will provide a strong foundation for learning to think together as a group of scientists.

This lesson creates opportunities for pupils briefly to experience different talk games and to reflect on their different purposes and the different, usually implicit rules that guide them. It leads into a deeper exploration of the game of Thinking Together in the second lesson.

Questions for reflection

- As you reflect on talk in your classroom, what different talk games can you identify?
- Have you considered teaching children the skills needed to play the different games? How could the Oracy Skills Framework support you to do this?
- Would it be a good idea to make the rules of each game explicit to support pupils from different backgrounds to join in? What cultural, physical, or developmental barriers might inhibit some of the children in your class?
- Do you – or could you – make the talk game best suited to a particular task explicit? "We're going to use a debate to test this out"; "We need to use some thinking together to work through this"; "Remember, this is a presentation you are giving"; "Which talk game do we need to play in this situation?"
- How could you use opportunities for presentation, debate, and thinking together to provide pupils with meaningful opportunities to apply subject-specific vocabulary?

Lesson 1

Notes for the busy teacher

Learning aim: I can list some different kinds of talk and explain why each can be useful

In this session, pupils are introduced to different modes or uses of talk. They are offered the analogy of different modes of talk as different games with different aims, rules, and skills. There is no authoritative taxonomy of such games, and this lesson suggests four common examples under the following headings: presentation (or monologue), debate, chat, and thinking together. The lesson gives pupils the opportunity to experience each talk game in a deliberate and conscious way to enable them to reflect on the purpose/value of the talk and the unwritten rules that it follows. Thinking together might be acknowledged as being particularly useful for learning in a group, and the pupils will explore this game in more depth in the next lesson.

Session plan

Skills building exercise (warm-up)

- Today we are going to talk about talk! Talking together often involves **responding** to what others have said (much as you might respond to another player's move in a game).

- Put the pupils in pairs. They are going to work together to create the opening sentence of a story. One person will contribute the opening word ("Once," for example), and the other will respond with the next word. They will continue to alternate until the sentence is complete.
- For extra challenge, tell pupils that their sentence needs to end on the 10th or 15th word. The exercise can be done as a whole class, with each pupil contributing a word (this may become a paragraph rather than a sentence!).
- You might then challenge the pairs or the class to construct another sentence, this time beginning with the stem, "Talk is important because…."
- Were the pupils able to respond effectively to their partners so that the sentences made sense? What did they notice about the way they needed to listen? Could they hear an inner voice predicting where the sentence was headed? Was there a conflict between listening to this and listening to their partner? Does this happen during real conversations too? Is responding to another person's moves in this way a bit like playing a game?

Stimulus and discussion

- Read "The games we play" to or with the class.
- Discuss the story with the children, making use of the discussion plan provided as appropriate. Do the pupils have questions in response to the story? These could be addressed now or collected and addressed later in the lesson.

Exercise

Tell the class that they are going to briefly experience four different talk games. They will be asked to reflect on each using a PMU method (i.e., they will be asked for the pluses, minuses, and uses of each game). The following sentence stems could be useful:

P: "It was good because..."
M: "It was hard to..."
U: "We could use this kind of talk when..."

Pupils will also be asked to reflect on the unwritten rules that guide each game.

Show images representing the different games (see supporting slide) and ask pupils to match each image to the appropriate label.

Presentation (or monologue)

- Place the class in groups of three and ask them to choose one person to speak from each group. That person will be asked to speak for one minute. They will speak more fluently and engagingly on a topic that is meaningful to them – a hobby or a book they have been reading, for example.
- Give the speakers some thinking time, and then give them one minute to speak.
- At the end of the minute, ask the pupils to talk about their PMUs. Gather some PMUs from different groups and list them on the board.

P: Pupils might say things like, "It's interesting to listen carefully to someone, especially if they tell a good story," and, "It's nice to be listened to."

M: They might also say, "It's frustrating not to be able to respond, or to have a turn."

U: Uses might include giving explanations or instructions or telling stories.

- Now ask the pupils for one or two rules that might guide this game. You might expect ideas around only one person speaking, listening quietly, saving any questions until the end, and so on.

Debate

- Tell the class that in this game each person or team is trying to convince the other that they are right. Place them in groups of four (one or two groups of five may be necessary; threes should be avoided). Each group should split into two teams of two (or a three and a two).
- Show them the statement, "Talking is more important than writing when you are learning." The first group has one minute to try to convince the others that the statement is true. The second group then has one minute to respond and convince the others that the statement is false. At the end of the exercise, collect the PMUs, which might include:

P: This was fun; it was a good way of testing different points of view.

M: You don't really listen to the others, or you only listen so that you can disagree; nobody really listens to you.

U: Giving people the chance to hear different arguments expressed strongly so that they can see which seems best – as seen in parliament and in courtrooms; teaching people to argue well.

- Now ask the pupils for one or two rules that might guide this kind of talk. You might expect ideas around never admitting when you are wrong, giving strong reasons to justify a position, and so on.

Chat

- Tell the class that this is a free-flowing discussion. Place them in groups of three.
- Encourage them to chat about what they have made of the lesson (or the day) so far. Allow about two minutes.
- Collect PMUs and rules as before. They might say things like, "Chat is easier," or "Chat is fun." You could point out that chat helps to build relationships, though it doesn't often lead to any conclusions or formal learning. There are unwritten rules – keep it interesting and fun, for example – and not everyone finds them easy to follow, which can lead to people not feeling included.

Thinking together

- Tell the class that this kind of talk involves exploring different ideas as we look for a better understanding or try to agree what is best to think or do. Place them in groups of three again, and pose the question, "Do mobile phones make us worse at communicating with each other?"

- Tell the group that they should try to agree on the three most important things said and write them down.
- Allow a little longer for this task (around five minutes) before taking PMUs. These might include:

P: "We get to hear different ideas"; "We get to share our own thoughts".
M: "It's frustrating not to have the right answer"; "Everyone was trying to talk at once".
U: "It's useful to think together as a team rather than relying on your own ideas".

- This will lead into a discussion of possible rules (speak one at a time and listen to everyone, for example); keep this brief today but make a note of the ideas shared and keep them for the next lesson.

Whole-class plenary

- Give the class some time to think back over the lesson. Can they summarise their main "take-away" in a headline?
- Is it useful to compare different kinds of talk to different games with different rules? What are the strengths and weaknesses of the analogy?
- Do we need to learn the rules and to practise using them, or does this come naturally?
- What about "thinking together"? Are we naturally good at this? Do we always talk well in groups? (You could use the final slide to stimulate some thinking together about this.)

- Share a conclusion like: "This kind of talk can be really useful, but it's not always easy, and well-thought-out rules will be needed." The class will work together to develop these next time.

Metacognition

- At the beginning of the lesson, the children practised responding to each other. How well did they respond to others for the rest of the lesson? Can they think of examples? What's the difference between waiting your turn to speak and responding?
- What other skills might the class need to practise if they are going to play the thinking together game well?

Resources

- Slide set to support the session
- Teachers wishing to explore the skills needed for different modes of communication in more detail may find it useful to explore the Oracy Skills Framework (see note 4 at the end of this chapter).

Vocabulary

Talk games: different ways of using talk in different situations.
Presentation: an extended speech by one person. This is more formally called a monologue. It can involve monological thinking if the speaker assumes that there is just one valid point of view.

Debate: a formal discussion on a particular matter, in which opposing arguments are put forward and which often ends with a vote.
Chat: an informal conversation.
Thinking together: using talk to think out loud in collaboration with others. Talk is focused on shared inquiry, asking questions, explaining, justifying, exploring alternatives, and generally seeking to understand the other participants' perspectives and the topic at hand. It involves dialogical thinking if multiple perspectives are allowed to interact.

Stimulus: The games we play

It was the first day of the school year at Newton Primary. Galileo class sat quietly as their new teacher, Mr Robins, called the register. After he'd finished, they kept sitting there quietly. It was strange being in a new class with a new teacher, and no one was sure what to say.

Mr Robins looked at them all with a frowning sort of smile. "You're all very quiet," he said, as he stood up and came out from behind his desk. "The first thing we are going to have to do is teach you to talk."

"We do know how to talk, Mr Robins!" Grace exclaimed. "We're just – you know – not sure what the rules are."

"Rules?" Mr Robins looked puzzled.

"Yes – we need to know when we're allowed to talk, and who to, and that sort of thing – then we know what we're doing," Grace explained.

"What do you think the rules should be?"

"We only speak when you ask us to?" offered Charlie B.

"Yes, and then we only speak one at a time," Bertie added.

"And most of the time we listen to you," said Ama.

"You make it all sound like a game!" Mr Robins laughed and then looked thoughtful. "Maybe we do play games and follow rules when we talk to each other," he said, "but perhaps there is more than one game and more than one set of rules. Perhaps we do need to learn how to talk together after all."

"Now I'm confused," said Grace.

"Well, I'm just thinking that there might be different kinds of talk or at least different ways of using talk in different situations," Mr Robins explained. "And maybe each is a different kind of game, with different rules. What do you think?"

Discussion plan

- Can you think of different uses of talk? Giving speeches might be one example. Having arguments or having a chat could be others. (See the distinction made between these uses of talk and a "way of talking" below.)
- In what ways are these different uses of talk like games? Do we "play" with or against someone, for example? Do we have to respond to the moves our fellow players make? Is there an objective or aim?
- Do the different talk games have different rules?
- Is there a difference between a talk game and a way of talking? For example, between giving a presentation and shouting? (It may be useful to make separate lists of talk games and ways of talking.)

- Are some ways of talking particularly helpful for some talk games? Using a soft tone in a chat or an assertive tone in a debate, for example. Are there other ways in which we behave differently in different talk games?

Notes

1 Ludwig Wittgenstein. *Philosophical Investigations*, 4th ed., trans. G.E.M. Anscombe, P.M.S. Hacker and Joachim Schulte (Wiley-Blackwell, 2009).

2 Mikhail M. Bakhtin. *Speech Genres and Other Late Essays*, ed. Caryl Emerson and Michael Holquist, trans. Vern W. McGee (University of Texas Press, 1986).

3 There is no authoritative taxonomy of modes of communication. The UK's Oracy Education Commission suggests four modes of talk in its final report: building understanding, debating and persuading, negotiating and making change, and expressing and performing. The Academy of Professional Dialogue refers to eight modes of communication. See: Oracy Education Commission. *We Need to Talk: The Report of the Commission on the Future of Oracy Education in England* (Voice 21 and Impetus, 2024), 32. Accessed November 2025. https://oracyeducationcommission.co.uk/wp-content/uploads/2024/10/We-need-to-talk-2024.pdf

4 University of Cambridge and School 21. *The Oracy Skills Framework*. 2018. PDF. Accessed November 2025. https://www.educ.cam.ac.uk/research/programmes/oracytoolkit/oracyskillsframework/Oracy%20Skills%20Framework%202020.pdf

2

Thinking together

The rules of the game

Notes for the curious teacher

In this lesson we turn our attention to one particular talk game — that of Thinking Together — and to the question of how we can help pupils learn to play it. One way to do this is by establishing and using clear ground rules.

What is "thinking together"?

The concept of "thinking together" is closely associated with the work of Neil Mercer, Rupert Wegerif, and Lyn Dawes in the 1990s.[1] Their research focused on how pupils use language to solve problems collaboratively. They noticed that in the most successful groups, pupils tended to:

 DOI: 10.4324/9781003663454-3

- share relevant information;
- engage critically but constructively with each other's ideas;
- give reasons for their ideas;
- actively participate;
- check their understanding by asking questions;
- build on each other's responses;
- strive for agreement.

These behaviours reflect what Mercer and his colleagues called *exploratory talk*, a concept first introduced by the classroom researcher, Douglas Barnes, in the 1970s. Barnes distinguished exploratory talk from *presentational talk* – the use of language to communicate polished conclusions to an audience. Exploratory talk sounds quite different from presentational talk: it is characterised by hesitations, rephrasings, false starts, and changes of direction. This form of talk allows pupils to think aloud, question, and collaboratively shape understanding, which Barnes felt to be crucial components of meaningful learning.

The use of exploratory talk enables *thinking together*: a talk game in which two or more perspectives are heard, valued, and used to create better understanding. Thinking together is a term that's accessible to young people and describes what we're encouraging them to do: we want them to use exploratory talk to think out loud so that they can collaborate to solve problems. With practice, pupils learn to use exploratory talk more confidently and to engage in thinking together more effectively.

It doesn't seem unreasonable to suggest that the success of science may owe much to the scientific community's ability to think together. This is true in the everyday sense that scientists must collaborate effectively in teams. But it's also true more fundamentally: over time, scientific progress depends on behaviours like those listed previously — openly sharing relevant information, offering reasons and evidence, responding to and building on others' ideas, and respectfully testing and challenging claims. Perhaps most important of all, scientists must remain open to the possibility that their current knowledge is provisional and may eventually be revised or replaced.

Why are ground rules important?

Mercer, Wegerif, and Dawes observed that pupils who were engaging in successful exploratory talk seemed to be following a set of implicit rules that shaped the way they interacted: "We should join in and share our thoughts" and "We should respond to what other people say," for example.

However, they found that most groups struggled to engage in this kind of talk without guidance. Some seemed more concerned with the harmony of the group than with solving the problems they had been set. It was as if they were following implicit rules such as, "We should always agree with our friends." This led to talk that was labelled as cumulative because it ended in uncritical agreement.

In other groups, pupils seemed focused on winning arguments. The implicit rules here might have been along the lines of, "Don't admit that you're wrong" or "Interrupt someone if you think they disagree with you." This led to talk that was labelled as disputational because it was competitive and adversarial.

It seemed to Mercer, Wegerif, and Dawes that the rules that guide effective exploratory talk should be made explicit. They referred to these rules as ground rules – a term that was used in the nineteenth century for rules that were particular to different baseball grounds, but is now taken to mean basic principles that set the framework for an activity – in this case for exploratory talk. They went on to gather a wealth of evidence to show that the use of ground rules to help pupils to move beyond unproductive talk patterns can have a transformative impact on their ability to collaborate.[2]

Rules as signposts

Some educators may feel uneasy about the term "rules," perhaps because it invokes strict regulations like, "Keep off the grass!" Philosopher Nicholas Burbules offers a helpful perspective, drawing on Wittgenstein's idea that rules act as signposts rather than fixed commands.[3] They help us to understand how to carry on as the game unfolds but allow flexibility and can be adapted to context as participants develop judgement and come to understand the spirit of the game.

This view of rules as signposts that guide us, but do not dictate to us with inflexible authority, makes them seem empowering rather than restrictive. The hope is that they eventually become internalised – transformed from external instructions to shared habits of mind. You will find them to be a powerful tool for teaching pupils to think together.

Making ground rules work

To make ground rules effective, it's helpful for teachers and pupils to co-create them so that they are meaningful and relevant to all. This lesson provides a practical guide to working with your pupils to establish ground rules that will enable pupils to engage with the activities in the remainder of the book through thoughtful, respectful collaboration.

Being able to suggest ground rules isn't the same as being confident to use them; it's important to consider how you can teach pupils to enact the behaviours (or, to continue the game analogy, "moves") described by the ground rules. In this book, each lesson begins with an activity aimed at allowing pupils to practise a "focus" behaviour or skill; lessons end with an opportunity to reflect on their use of the focus skill and on its value. The hope is that this will enable a greater metacognitive awareness of the skills of the Thinking Together game.

We very much hope that the impact of your ground rules will extend well beyond their use in the TTiPS lessons.

Questions for reflection

- What do you understand by the term "thinking together"? How does it differ from simply talking together? How would you explain it to someone who was unclear of its meaning?
- How often do you experience this kind of communication in your own life? When it happens, what makes it possible?
- How often do you hear good thinking together in your classroom? Do you hear cumulative and disputational talk?
- What implicit rules do your pupils seem to follow when they talk together?
- What ground rules would you suggest for them?
- Being able to suggest ground rules isn't the same as being confident to use them. How could you teach the behaviours or "moves" set out in your class's ground rules? Do you think they will be useful across the curriculum?

Lesson 2

Notes for the busy teacher

Learning aim: I can use a set of ground rules to help me to explain how to "think together"

Thinking together means using talk to think out loud in collaboration with others. In this session pupils will explore this talk game in more detail. Thinking together can be particularly helpful when trying to understand difficult ideas or solve problems. But talking in this way doesn't come as easily as we might hope – we need to learn how to do it. One way to support that learning process is to establish some norms for effective thinking together through a set of ground rules (just as rules in other games provide structure and help us know how to behave or carry on). Once established, these rules can be used as a guide and as a tool for reflection and metacognition. By the end of the lesson, your class will have constructed a (provisional) set of ground rules for use in the subsequent lessons (and, we hope, in all lessons!). There is good evidence to show that the use of ground rules as a guide can significantly enhance classroom dialogue.

Session plan

Skills building exercise (warm-up)

- In the last lesson, the pupils practised responding to each other. Implicit in that exercise was listening carefully, a skill that they will now practise further.
- Place the class in pairs and tell them that one of them will speak for a minute on a subject of personal interest. An example might be *My hopes for the future*. Try to choose a topic that requires a personal response, as this will encourage attentive listening.
- The second pupil will listen carefully, giving feedback on the things they found interesting ("I was interested in…"), and, if possible, asking a question that calls for elaboration on a particular point ("Can you tell me more about…?"). They should avoid using the feedback as an opportunity to speak about themselves.
- Give the pupils time to prepare. The speaker could make a few notes — bullet points, not a script. The listener can reflect on what *careful listening* might involve.
- Time one minute for speaking and 30 seconds to a minute for feedback and the follow-up question.
- If time allows, the roles can be reversed.
- Give the pairs a minute to reflect together on what careful listening is, then take some feedback. It might be useful to explore meanings of the word *care* (the word is associated with empathy and kindness, but its root meanings include concern and interest, serious mental attention, and curiosity or the desire to understand). Good listening involves having a particular attitude or orientation towards the other person.

Stimulus and discussion

- Read "Thinking together – the rules of the game" to or with the class.
- Discuss the story with the children, making use of the discussion plan provided as appropriate. Do the pupils have questions in response to the story? These could be addressed now or collected and addressed later in the lesson.

Main exercise

- The class is going to think together(!!) to construct and agree a set of rules for thinking together.
- Place the class in groups of three and provide each group with a piece of paper and five to seven large Post-it® notes (or use a digital tool such as Talkwall, Padlet, or an online collaborative whiteboard. This would probably lead to a more effective plenary session).
- Display the sentence stem, "Thinking together works well when we ...." Give the class some silent thinking time so that each pupil can think back over their experience of thinking together in the last session, and their experience of the story in this session, and consider what behaviours would support effective thinking together.
- Ask each pupil in turn to suggest a ground rule to their group and to explain why they think it would be useful. Remind pupils of the discussion about careful listening and its value. Give each pupil two opportunities to share. Each suggested ground rule should be recorded on the piece of paper.

- Now ask the group to try to agree on an order of importance for their rules (again, emphasise the importance of careful listening). This will help them discuss the value of each rule in more depth.
- Give them a short time to reflect on the activity – the way they have talked together and the rules they have suggested. Are there rules that they have missed?
- Ask each group to write the two most important ground rules on separate Post-it notes. They should make their writing as large as possible, so that it can be seen from a distance.
- On a third note, they should write a rule they regard as important but perhaps less obvious – something others might not have considered.
- Collect the Post-it notes on a display board (or invite the students to post their rules on the digital platform).

Whole-class plenary

- Gather the pupils around the Post-it-note display (seating them in a horseshoe around the screen would work well if using a digital platform).
- Can they see rules that are the same or similar? Could these be grouped together? How could the rule they suggest be expressed best?
- Are there other rules that only one group has suggested, but are nevertheless valuable?
- Make a list of the agreed rules. Ideally, this will contain between five and ten rules. Any more than this and it may be useful to prioritise or combine similar rules.

- Are the class happy with the rules and the wording of them? If someone else came into the room at this point, what rule might they suggest that the class has missed?
- Look at suggested ground rules in the accompanying slide set. Are any of these not represented? Perhaps you could suggest adding one or two of them.
- Make a judgement as to whether you have too many rules to be useful, and if so, engage in further revision — try to get the list down to around eight rules.
- The class will use these ground rules to guide them in thinking together in future lessons. They are provisional — the class might decide to change them or add to them as time goes on.

Please note: You might find it useful to print copies of the rules so that each group can have a set on their table during subsequent lessons. It may not be worth laminating them just yet, as they should remain open to revision.

Metacognition

- How *carefully* did pupils listen to each other today? Can anyone share an example of a moment in which they felt they were listened to or not listened to? Why is careful listening important?
- How carefully did *you*, the teacher, listen to the children? Can you reflect on examples? How can you develop your own listening?
- Of the rules suggested today, which do the class do well? Which might they need to focus on in future lessons?

Resources

- Slide set to support the session
- Paper and large Post-it notes, or a digital platform to facilitate the collaborative compilation of the ground rules (Talkwall, Padlet, and Jamboard are examples)

Talk prompts and vocabulary

Talk prompts

For this lesson's thinking together focus: "I was interested in…"; "Can you tell me more about…"; "Thank you for sharing…."

Vocabulary

Thinking together: talk is focused on shared inquiry, asking questions, explaining, justifying, exploring alternatives, and generally seeking to understand the other participants' perspectives and the topic at hand. It involves dialogical thinking if multiple perspectives are allowed to interact. **Or, for children**, using talk to think out loud in a team.

Ground rules: the norms of behaviour in this kind of interaction, **or, for children**, a set of rules that helps us to understand how to play the Thinking Together game.

Careful listening: the word "care" is associated with empathy and kindness, but its root meanings include concern and interest, serious mental attention, and curiosity or the desire to understand.

Stimulus: Thinking together – the rules of the game

"So, what kind of talking game are we going to play today, Mr Robins?" asked Charlie T.

Galileo class had been talking about talk at the beginning of the new school year. Mr Robins had introduced them to different uses of talk and suggested that they were a bit like games with different rules. "Well, Charlie," Mr Robins replied, "which one do we think would be most useful for us to practise as a class?"

"Chatting!" exclaimed Molly-with-a-y. "It stops us getting bored – and it helps us to be friendly."

"Don't be stupid, Molly!" snapped Tala. "We already know how to chat, and it isn't going to help us to learn anything."

"Tala, you are free to disagree with Molly, or with anyone else, but please be respectful. Molly has a point when she says that chat is useful, so kindly value what she has to say." Mr Robins had put on his serious and slightly cross voice.

"Sorry, Molly," Tala said, sounding sincere. "But wouldn't it be more useful for us to learn how to debate ideas?"

"Give us a reason for that, Tala – why should we spend time learning to debate?" Mr Robins asked. To Tala's relief, he now sounded more interested than cross.

"Well, it teaches us to be good at arguing and, well, persuading people and stuff."

Now Mr Robins stayed silent, holding his arms out to the class as an invitation to carry on.

"Yeah, I agree with Tala," said Karl, "because we need to be able to speak confidently in front of people."

"I think Molly and Tala and Karl all have good points." It was Charlie B's turn to speak up. "But I think we'll learn most if we do that 'thinking together' thing, because… well… you know." Charlie seemed to run out of words, but Grace was quick to help him out.

"Yes, Charlie," she said, "I think it helps you to understand more."

"Because you get to hear what other people are thinking, you mean?" asked Tala, who was looking more and more interested.

"Well, yes, but talking helps you to understand too." Grace saw that people were looking puzzled, so, after thinking for a short while, she went on, "Sometimes I think I've understood what the teacher is saying, but when I try to say it out loud I can't."

"So, talking just made things worse!" said Molly-with-a-y.

"Well, I know what you mean, but I don't think so. If I can't put it into words, then I probably don't quite understand it," said Grace. "At least when I try, I realise there's a problem."

"Yes, I agree with you, Grace," Ama joined in. "Then you can ask someone else if they can explain it – or sometimes they sort of help you to… you know."

"Finish your sentence?" offered Karl.

Mr Robins laughed. "You know what? I think you are thinking together already! I wonder if we can figure out what makes thinking together work."

Discussion plan

- Do you agree with Mr Robins when he says that the class was thinking together? What evidence can we see in their talk?

- What did Mr Robins mean when he said that Tala should "value" what Molly had to say?
- Is it rude to disagree with someone?
- How do you feel when people disagree with you? Can it be helpful? Does it always seem helpful at the time?
- Why didn't Mr Robins just tell the class which type of talk was most useful for them?
- If teachers explain things carefully, why would talking help you to understand?
- Do you think that thinking together is useful in school? In what ways might it be useful?
- In the last lesson, you suggested some rules for thinking together. Can you remember what they were? (If necessary, share the notes made in the last lesson).
- Are there other rules that would be helpful?

Notes

1 Lyn Dawes, Neil Mercer, and Rupert Wegerif. *Thinking Together: A Programme of Activities for Developing Speaking, Listening and Thinking Skills for Children Aged 8–11*, 2nd ed. (Imaginative Minds, 2004).

2 University of Cambridge. "Thinking Together Project." Accessed November 2025. https://thinkingtogether.educ.cam.ac.uk/

3 Nicholas C. Burbules. *Dialogue in Teaching: Theory and Practice* (Teachers College Press, 1993).

3

Bertie's Kite

Notes for the curious teacher

In this chapter, and in those that follow, we turn our attention to science. We'll get the children thinking together about some scientific ways of thinking and about any implications for the trust they place in scientists and their work. We'll make connections between scientific thinking and everyday thinking, particularly in relation to misinformation. But first, we should ask ourselves — and the children — some basic questions about what science is and is not.

What is science?

Let's begin by clearing up a common misunderstanding: science is not simply a collection of facts about the world that children

 DOI: 10.4324/9781003663454-4

need to memorise! It's much more than that. Science is a way — or rather a family of related ways — of finding things out about the world. Importantly, the knowledge that has been gathered in this way is not final — it's always open to revision and change.

It's worth emphasising this because it helps us frame science education in a way that's appealing — even exciting — for children. Science is not complete! Our children can aspire to play a part in its unfolding story, and all of them can benefit from learning about this way of finding out and from using it to explore their own questions and experiences.

We should also stress that science is not the only way of finding out about the world. People use storytelling, philosophy, art, religion, and personal experience to make sense of their lives. These different ways of knowing often deal with questions that science isn't capable of answering directly — especially questions about meaning, value, or purpose.

So, how can we characterise science as a particular way of knowing?

Science is empirical

Firstly, science is a way of finding out about the world by gathering evidence through our senses, often with the help of tools and instruments. Observation, measurement, and experiment are key features of scientific activity. In other words, science is **empirical**.

It's important to stress that not all science involves formal experiments. In some fields, like astronomy or geology, scientists observe, measure, and make careful inferences from the evidence they can find. But ultimately, if we claim to know something about the world that can't be tested by observation, measurement, or experiment, then we're not being scientific.

This means that scientists can't rely on their instinct or "gut feeling" to tell them about the way things are. Nor can they rely solely on reason, logic, or theory — their ideas must eventually connect with testable evidence.

Science is rational

That's not to say that gut feelings and reasoning aren't useful to scientists — they often are. Indeed, **rational thinking** is essential for making sense of the evidence that's gathered. Scientists use different forms of reason to look for patterns, think about causes and effects, test explanations, and make predictions. We'll explore these forms of reasoning in future chapters.

One form of rational thinking is particularly important: staying open to new evidence. This can be difficult, especially when the evidence challenges — or even overturns — ideas a person has held onto. Scientific knowledge is never certain — it's based on the best available evidence, and scientists are always testing it. When new evidence comes to light — and has been checked rigorously by the scientific community — theories and accepted knowledge may need to change.

This is precisely why we can present science as a continually unfolding story that draws in new authors from every generation.

Science is human

It would be easy to imagine scientists as completely — coldly — rational, a bit like computers. But of course, they are human beings and are susceptible to the full range of human emotions, biases, and motivations — they are certainly not always rational. This can cause trouble. For example, individual scientists don't always like having their theories challenged and changed, and they can be tempted to turn a blind eye to inconvenient evidence, or even to wilfully mislead people.

This is why the scientific community is so important. Through processes such as peer review and replication, it helps ensure that the values of empiricism and rationality are brought to bear over time. So, the ability to think together with a wider community is essential for good science — as we'll see in later chapters.

And those human qualities aren't all problematic — far from it. Abilities such as empathy, teamwork, creativity, and perseverance are as vital in science as they are in other fields.

So, science is empirical, it's rational, and it's human. In this lesson, children will have a first opportunity to think about these ideas through reflection on a story and in response to a practical challenge. The lesson should enable them to list terms such as observation, measurement, testing, and experiment as part of what makes science, science.

Questions for reflection

- How does this characterisation of science fit with your own conception of it? Has your own answer to the question "What is science?" changed in any way?
- Do you think it's important to understand science as a way of knowing as well as a body of knowledge? Why?
- What do you make of claims that scientific knowledge is never certain, never final, and incomplete? Could an appreciation of these things change the way people think of science? How could it change the way young people relate to it?
- As you reflect on your own day-to-day life, do you think you think and behave in a scientific way at times? How so? What about the children in your class? Do they behave as scientists sometimes?

- How might an understanding of science as an open-ended, evidence-based, rational, and human process help children critically evaluate information they encounter?
- As you reflect on the way science is taught in school, do you think it would be beneficial to place more emphasis on the ways in which scientists think and work? What would the impact of this be?

Lesson 3

Notes for the busy teacher

Learning aim: I can list some of the things that make science, science

This lesson sets out to get children thinking about what distinguishes science from other ways of learning about the world. Scientists rely on empirical evidence – that is to say that their beliefs, hypotheses, and theories are based on observation, measurement, and experiment. In the stimulus, Tala prefers to rely on her intuition (the ability to understand something instinctively, perhaps through a "gut feeling," without the need for conscious reasoning); she says things like, "Just do what feels right," and "If it looks right, it is right." Molli, on the other hand, takes a rationalist approach (she prefers to rely on theoretical understanding and logical thinking without the need for testing/ experimentation). Bertie takes on board Molli's theoretical ideas (rational thinking is certainly valuable in science), but he wants to test them and gather empirical evidence through experiments – he is behaving as a scientist. Discussion of the stimulus and reflection on the exercise should enable pupils to list terms such as observation, measurement, testing, and experiment as part of what makes science, science.

Session plan

Skills building exercise (warm-up)

Remind the pupils of their ground rules and that, in the introductory lessons, they explored the skills of responding and listening. Another important skill in group work is making sure that everyone is included — they have a chance to speak and be listened to. In this activity, everyone will get a turn to talk and everyone else will practise listening:

- Put the class into groups of five or six and seat them in circles. (This activity could be done as a whole class if preferred, though it would take longer.)
- Introduce the "talking stick" as a special object that helps them remember who is talking (any object will do!).
- Only the person holding the talking stick is allowed to speak. Once they are finished, they should pass it on to the next person in the circle.
- Provide sentence stems for each round of talk. Perhaps the first one or two will be easily accessible and fun: "Something you don't know about me is…"; "Something good that has happened to me recently is…"; "Something I am proud of is…."

- You could then move onto stems such as, "What I like about science is..."; "The most interesting sciency thing I know is..."; "You know when you are doing science because..."; "What makes science, science is...."
- People should be encouraged to speak — most importantly through the body language of the listeners, who show their interest. But they should also have the right to "pass the stick" if nothing comes to mind. It's important to create a safe space that enables risk taking — for some pupils, it will take a while before they feel able to take a risk.
- After everyone has had a turn, talk about how it felt to speak and listen.
- Discuss why it's important to include everyone in conversations. Ask, "How did it feel when everyone listened to you?" and "How did it feel when you listened to others?"; "What did you hear that was interesting?"; "What did you hear that no-one else could have said?"
- The group might think it worthwhile introducing a "talking stick" whenever they are working in groups of three or more, to help them to include everyone.

Stimulus and discussion

- Read Bertie's Kite to the class.
- Discuss the story with the children, making use of the discussion plan provided as appropriate. Do the pupils have questions in response to the story? These could be addressed now or collected and addressed following the main activity.

Main exercise

Note: If you don't have the space to fly paper planes, a similar exercise could be done with "spinners" with the children attempting to make the fastest spinner. The key is for them to recognise that they are being scientists by observing, measuring, experimenting, and making reasoned modifications – just like Bertie!

- Put the class into pairs and explain that they will be thinking together to design a paper plane that can fly as far as possible.
- Demonstrate one way of making a paper plane, perhaps using the instructions included in the accompanying slide set.
- Give each pair a piece of paper. You could vary the size and thickness of the paper so that, when pairs later combine into groups of four, their planes will inevitably differ in some ways.
- Give the pairs a few minutes to think together about their design and to make their plane. They may use the instructions included in the slides as a guide, but they don't have to. **They should not throw the plane yet!**
- Ask the pairs to join with another pair to make groups of four. Would a talking stick support them to include everyone in their group talk? Some of the following talk prompts might also help.
- Invite the groups to compare their two planes and think together to make a prediction about which will fly the furthest. What does their intuition (gut feeling) tell them? Do they have reasons to support their

predictions? You could support them with some "target vocabulary" such as wing, shape, size, weight, streamlined, air resistance, nose, lift, tail, and so on.

- Now, with appropriate attention to safety, allow the groups to test their planes. Encourage them to observe or measure (simple forms of measurement are fine) the distances flown. (You might briefly discuss controlling variables such as the thrower or the strength of throw, but there's no need to worry too much about this for the purposes of this lesson.)
- Invite the groups to think together again. Were their predictions correct? Can they modify the design of their "winning" plane so that it would fly even further? What would they change and why? Are they drawing on intuition, or using reasoning? Allow them time to make a modified plane.
- Do they feel confident that this new plane will fly further? Can they be certain? How should they find out? Allow them to test the new planes, comparing the distance flown with that flown by the previous model.
- Ask the groups to reflect together on their efforts. Was the new design a success? What have they learned? What would they change next?
- Finally, ask them to reflect on a bigger question: have they been behaving like scientists? In what ways?

Whole-class plenary

The children worked as scientists because they tested their designs experimentally, making measurements, observations, and systematic, reasoned changes.

Pupils may remember that the class featured in the stories in this book is called "Galileo class". The class is named after Galileo Galilei, who was born in the sixteenth century. Some people say that he was the first modern scientist. Show the final slide in which Aristotle, Galileo, and Cremonini speak about the heavenly bodies. Tell the children that Cesare Cremonini and Galileo were teachers at the same university in Padua, Italy. They were friends but often disagreed! Cremonini strongly believed in the teachings of the great Greek philosopher, Aristotle, who had lived more than a thousand years before them.

Having explored the slide, ask the children to think about why Galileo might have been described as a scientist. How is his approach different from those of the other two characters? It's said that Cremonini refused to look through the telescope. Why might this have been? Why didn't Aristotle look through a telescope? In fact, the telescope was invented in 1608. The invention of new instruments like the telescope at this time enabled more accurate observations and measurements and led to the "scientific revolution" and the growth of modern science.

Metacognition

Give the groups of three time to think together around the following questions:

- Was everyone included in our talk and in our activities today? How does this help to increase the quality of the thinking together?

- Which other rules did the groups do well with? Why were they useful?
- Are there rules they need to focus on more next time? How will they help?

Resources

- Slide set to support the session
- Paper for creating paper planes
- Measuring equipment suitable for measuring the length of flight of a paper plane (this might be limited to some way of marking on the ground where the plane landed)
- Space for flying paper planes

Talk prompts and vocabulary

Talk prompts

For this lesson's thinking together focus: "What do you think, X…?"; "Does anyone else have something to share?"

For this lesson's thinking scientifically focus: "I think this one will fly further… because…"; "We could change…"; "I think that change would / wouldn't work because…"; "We were working like scientists when we…."

Vocabulary

Intuitive: based on instinct — perhaps a "gut feeling" — without the need for conscious reasoning.

Rational: based on reason and logical thinking.

Empirical: based on evidence gathered through the senses (sometimes using tools or instruments). Observation, measurement, and experiment are typical features of scientific work.

Observation: the act of noticing or paying attention to something through direct experience, usually using the senses.

Measurement: the process of finding out the size or quantity of something (its length, weight, or temperature, for example) and expressing it with a number.

Experiment: a test done to find something out, or to check whether an idea works or is true. (Interestingly, the word shares a root with *experience* – the Latin *experiri* meaning to try or put to the test.)

Stimulus: Bertie's Kite

Bertie was worried about his homework. Galileo class had been making kites in their technology lessons, and Mr Robins had set them the task of adding a tail over the weekend. On Monday, they would all fly them together.

"Bertie! This is the funnest homework we've had in ages – how can you possibly be worried about it?" Tala asked him as they stood by the school gate before heading home.

"Well, how do I know how to make a good tail? What if I make one that's too long, or too heavy and it spoils my kite?"

"You're thinking too much, Bertie!" Tala seemed amused by Bertie's serious demeanour. "Just do what feels good – or looks nice. I'm going with great long yellow and pink ribbons woven together – it's going to look just fabulous!"

"Probably won't fly, though, Tala," said Molli-with-an-i.

"You see, the tail is needed so that your kite stays up straight. I've been reading about it, and the book I read said that the tail should be exactly four times as long as the kite itself and made out of something light but strong, like strips of old plastic bags. That's what I'll be doing."

"You are joking, aren't you?" asked Tala.

"Why?"

"Old plastic bags! It will look horrible!"

"Who cares as long as it flies well, Tala? What's the point of a nice-looking kite that turns upside down and crashes all the time?" Molli demanded.

"My kite won't crash," said Tala, confidently. "You trust books too much, Molli. I'll know when the tail's the right length: when it looks right, it is right!"

"And you trust your intuition too much, Tala! We'll see what we see on Monday." There was a confident twinkle in Molli's eye as she turned away and headed home.

"We will," Tala called after her, defiantly. "And at least my kite will be worth seeing. Old plastic bags indeed! See you tomorrow, Bertie." With that, she skipped away as if she just could not wait to start weaving her ribbons.

On Monday morning, Bertie was looking more cheerful as he passed his finished kite to Mr Robins; it had a simple tail made of bright orange fabric.

"You got it done then, Bertie – and it looks nice too," Tala whispered to him as he sat down.

"Thanks! It was hard work, though!" Bertie replied.

"Come on now, Bertie," Tala laughed. "It's only one strip of fabric – you should have seen all the weaving I had to do!"

"Ha! Mine took ten minutes," Molli boasted. "One strip of plastic, four times the length of the kite. Job done!"

That afternoon, Molli and Tala ran to catch up with Bertie as he set off home. "How did you do it, Bertie?" demanded Molli. "Your kite was the straightest and the highest and mine should have been best because it said so in the book!"

"Ah," smiled Bertie, "I heard what you said, Molli – about the length and material and all that, but I thought I should test it out."

"What do you mean?" asked Tala, whose kite, with its enormous, colourful ribbon, had failed to get more than two metres off the ground.

"I started with a plastic strip, as Molli suggested, and I tried five different lengths to see which kept the kite straightest. Then I tried different materials until I found the one that let it fly highest, which was the nice, light fabric. Last of all, I chose a colour that looked cool!"

"Bertie! You're such a little scientist!" laughed Tala.

Discussion plan

- The three children all took different approaches to making the tails for their kites. How would you describe Tala's approach?
- What might Tala have meant when she said, "When it looks right, it is right!"
- What could Molli have meant when she said that Tala trusted her intuition too much?
- Have you ever taken a similar approach to Tala? What were you doing, and how did it work out?
- If Tala's kite was the most beautiful, does it matter if it didn't fly so well? How would you decide which kite was best?

- What approach did Molli take?
- Why didn't Molli's approach work as well as she hoped? What could she have done differently?
- Why did Tala say that Bertie was "such a little scientist"?
- Do you think that Bertie was being more like a scientist than Tala or Molli? Why?
- Should you always take a scientific approach to solving problems?

4

Mrs Chestnut's duck

Notes for the curious teacher

Over the next three lessons, we'll explore three distinct kinds of reasoning commonly used by scientists to make and test hypotheses and to infer general rules. They are: abductive reasoning, deductive reasoning and inductive reasoning — or, put more accessibly: "Maybe…" thinking, "If… then… thinking" and, "So the rule is… thinking".

We'll begin by looking at abductive reasoning and its role in the creation of hypotheses.

What is a hypothesis?

It's September 1928. Alexander Fleming has returned to his laboratory after a holiday. He's been growing bacteria on

DOI: 10.4324/9781003663454-5

special plates so that he can study their properties, and he eagerly checks to see how they've grown while he's been away. He observes that one of his plates has been contaminated with a fungus. While some bacterial colonies are developing well on the plate, those near the fungus have been destroyed.

"That's funny!" Fleming exclaims. He wonders what's happened to the bacteria near the fungus (we should add curiosity to our list of human traits that benefit science!). "**Maybe** the fungus is producing a chemical that kills the bacteria," he suggests tentatively.

At this point, Fleming had limited evidence to support his idea – it was a kind of guess, and could well have been wrong. But it wasn't a wild guess. He already knew a great deal about bacteria, and he'd previously discovered that some of them could be killed by an enzyme found in mucus. No, this was an educated – or informed – guess.

Importantly, it was also a guess that could be tested. **If** the mould really was producing an antibacterial substance, Fleming reasoned, **then** it should kill a range of bacteria. He deliberately grew more of the contaminating mould and conducted experiments to test his idea. When he found that the mould could kill multiple strains of bacteria, he continued his experiments and called the antibacterial substance it produced penicillin. Penicillin was later developed into a medicine that revolutionised treatment and has saved countless lives. Fleming later shared the Nobel Prize for this work.

All this began with the observation of an unexpected phenomenon, followed by an educated guess about its cause – a guess that could be tested by experiment. Scientists call this kind of guess a **hypothesis**.

What is abductive reasoning?

It's not just scientists who make hypotheses. If you stepped outside this morning and found the grass to be wet, what might you think? You might suggest that it had rained recently. This isn't the only explanation you could offer – perhaps someone threw a bucket of water on the lawn, or your partner had been up early and put the sprinkler on. But, based on your past experience – and on what you know about your partner – rain seems to be the most plausible explanation.

This is an example of **abductive reasoning**: finding the most likely (and often the simplest) explanation for an observation. That's what Fleming did when he saw the dead bacteria. A number of explanations may have crossed his mind, but based on his knowledge and experience, the involvement of the fungus seemed the most likely. This kind of reasoning does require some creative thinking; contrary to popular belief, science is a creative discipline. It's important to remember, though, that the creative process should be constrained by relevant facts and knowledge.

Why is this important?

Hypothesis formation lies at the heart of scientific thinking. It allows scientists to make sense of puzzling observations by proposing possible explanations – ideas that can then be tested and refined. The most powerful scientific advances often begin with a well-formed hypothesis – a reasoned guess that provides a starting point for further inquiry. Hypothesis formation enables science not just to describe the world, but to ask, "What might be going on here?" and to pursue answers in a deliberate, imaginative, and systematic way.

In everyday life, too, abductive reasoning helps us to think carefully about the explanations we're offered – especially when we hear something surprising or suspicious. If we practise asking "What's the most likely explanation for this?" or "Could there be another reason?" we are less likely to be misled by dramatic headlines, internet rumours, or half-truths. Instead of jumping to conclusions, we learn to pause, ask questions, and consider what else might be going on. In this way, scientific thinking becomes not just a way to understand the natural world, but a powerful tool for navigating an information-rich – and sometimes misinformation-filled – world.

In this lesson, children will have the opportunity to practise abductive reasoning and hypothesis formation in both everyday and scientific contexts. You can talk about abductive reasoning with the children if you wish, but we have used the accessible term "Maybe..." thinking, because this kind of thinking is often vocalised with stems such as, "Maybe...," "What if...," or "It's as if...."

Questions for reflection

- Can you think of an example of a hypothesis you have made in everyday life? Could it be described as an educated guess that could be tested?
- Usually there's more than one possible explanation for an observation. In the example you just reflected on, what led you to settle on one particular explanation? What makes "a good guess" in your view?
- Think about the recent science topics you have taught. Can you think of examples of children being given opportunities to form and share a hypothesis to explain a surprising observation?

- Could you create more opportunities for this? How might children explain surprising observations such as plants growing towards the light, metals feeling cold to the touch, substances dissolving in water, a lunar eclipse, streamlined objects falling faster through water than non-streamlined objects, and so on?
- How might giving children opportunities to think together (using abductive reasoning) to form hypotheses benefit their science learning? Could it have everyday benefits too?
- We've used the term 'Maybe...' thinking because 'Maybe....' is a common way to begin a hypothesis. What other sentence stems would support your pupils to think abductively?

Lesson 4

Notes for the busy teacher

Learning aim: I can use "Maybe..." thinking to create a hypothesis

This session introduces children to abductive reasoning. This type of reasoning starts with an observation, and then a possible explanation (or hypothesis) is constructed around it. Where multiple explanations are possible, the one preferred should be simple, plausible, and consistent with the facts and existing knowledge. The process is a creative one – we've called it "Maybe..." thinking here, as language such as "Maybe..." or "It's as if..." or "Perhaps..." signifies that a creative suggestion is to follow. It's important to remember, though, that the creative process should be constrained by relevant facts and knowledge. The pupils should explore the distinction between a "wild guess" and an "informed guess." A hypothesis is the latter (scientists may resist the use of the word guess – they would certainly emphasise the *informed* part – but the word is not inaccurate and works well for children). It's important to note that a scientific hypothesis can and should be tested by further observation and experiment and then changed if necessary (just as Bertie tested Molli's suggestions about kite making in the previous lesson and modified her design). Many, though not all, scientific enquiries begin with an observation followed by abductive reasoning to form a hypothesis.

Session plan

Skills building exercise (warm-up)

Remind the pupils of their ground rules and the skills they have practised so far. An important part of thinking together is a willingness to share your ideas, even if you're not confident that they're "right." In this exercise, everyone should try to offer a suggestion using language such as "Maybe..." or "It's as if...." They should also listen carefully and respond by building on people's ideas, perhaps using language like, "Adding to/Building on what X said...".

- Place the pupils in groups of three and show them the image on Slide 2. What's happening here?
- Give the pupils some time to think, and then tell them that each person in the group should suggest an explanation. Use a talking stick if necessary (see Lesson 3).
- Encourage them to think together to decide which explanation seems best, or most likely.
- Invite some groups to share their explanations.
- Are we just guessing? Do some guesses seem more likely to be right than others? Why?
- Which one seems to offer the most likely explanation?
- Repeat with Slide 3. Do the pupils know anything about materials that might help to "inform" their guess?
- In the children's view, what makes a good guess?

Stimulus and discussion

- Read Mrs Chestnut's Duck to or with the class.
- Discuss the story with the children, making use of the discussion plan provided as appropriate. Do the pupils have questions in response to the story? These could be addressed now or collected and addressed following the main activity.

Main exercise

Just like the pupils during the warm-up, and the children in the story, scientists try to explain their observations of the natural world. They may find some clues, or evidence, to help them, but may not have enough evidence to be certain. They have to make an informed (or educated) guess when they suggest an explanation – they use "Maybe..." thinking!

A guess that is informed by scientific knowledge is a **hypothesis**. It can be tested by gathering further observations and evidence.

- Show the pupils the first part of Slide 7 (the mystery of the dying bacteria). Read the observation and connect it to the diagram.
- Can the pupils guess what might have happened? Allow them to think individually before thinking together in groups of three. Encourage everyone to share their ideas.
- Now show the clue or evidence and read it to the class. Give the pupils more time to think together. Does this make their guess more informed? Do they have a hypothesis now?
- Show the pupils the hypothesis on the slide and discuss the outcome. The mould got into the Petri dish by accident, but it was Fleming's careful observations and his ability to make an informed guess that led to the discovery of penicillin.
- You could continue to step the pupils through the exercise using the slides, or you could use the worksheet provided to allow the pupils to work in groups of three. The next two problems should be fairly familiar and might lead to hypotheses that could be tested in school. The final problems are examples from the history of science and should get the children thinking!
- Remind pupils to be guided by their rules and to encourage everyone to share an idea.

Whole-class plenary

Show the final slide, in which three children offer reasons for animals having camouflage. Discuss these with the pupils using the following guiding questions:

- **Could any of these guesses be called hypotheses? Why?**
  Reinforce the importance of making an informed guess that is consistent with the available evidence and isn't overly complicated. Sebi's guess isn't informed. Ama's explanation seems the most likely.
- **How should people like Sebi, Ama, and Karl – and scientists – respond when extra information and evidence shows that their guesses, or hypotheses, are wrong?**
  Emphasise that scientists should be open to changing their view if evidence shows their hypothesis to be wrong.
- **How does a hypothesis help us to solve a mystery (even if it turns out to be wrong)?**
  "Maybe…" thinking allows us to propose explanations for the things we observe. If we test these explanations and they are shown to be correct, the mystery is solved — for now at least. If they are shown to be incorrect, we have eliminated one possibility and can move on to a different explanation — we're a step closer to solving the mystery.

Metacognition

Give the groups of three time to think together around the following questions:

- Was everyone willing to share their ideas today? How did this affect the quality of the thinking together?
- Is "Maybe…" thinking useful when you're not certain of an answer or explanation?
- Which other rules did the groups do well with? Why were they useful?
- Are there rules they need to focus on more next time? How will they help?

Resources

- Slide set to support the session
- Pupil worksheet to support independent group work if desired

Talk prompts and vocabulary

Talk prompts

For this lesson's thinking together and working scientifically foci: "Maybe…"; "It's as if…"; "What if…."

Vocabulary

Abductive reasoning: thinking about the simplest and most likely conclusion from a set of observations, **or, for children** using "Maybe…" thinking to suggest explanations for surprising things you observe. (No need to mention the term "abductive reasoning" to the children if you prefer not to.)

Hypothesis: a proposed explanation made on the basis of limited evidence as a starting point for further investigation, **or, for children** an explanation for something surprising you observe that seems likely but isn't certain.

Explanation: a statement or account that makes something clear – for example, a scientist might explain the cause of a phenomenon.

Stimulus: Mrs Chestnut's duck

"I'll meet you under Mrs Chestnut's duck," yelled Grace as she ran into her classroom. She stopped dead: Mr Robins wasn't there. Instead there was a supply teacher; the name Mrs Jupiter was written on the board.

"Under what?" asked Mrs Jupiter. She looked a bit cross.

"Um… Mrs Chestnut's duck," answered Grace faintly.

"And what on earth is that?" asked Mrs Jupiter again, but with a smile this time.

"Oh!" said Grace, brightening.

"There's a big tree by the fence and it has an enormous rubber duck stuck up in the branches – it's like, bigger than a football, it's always been there. Well, the house behind the fence belongs to Mrs Chestnut, and she bought the duck on the internet for her cat, Mr Paw, but she didn't know it was a giant one. Mr Paw was petrified when he saw it, and Mrs Chestnut didn't know what to do, so she threw it out of her bedroom window. It got stuck up in the tree and it's been there ever since."

Mrs Jupiter had a slightly glazed look in her eyes by the end of Grace's explanation. Sebi didn't: he was giggling at Grace.

"Grace," he said, in between giggles,

"you do know that's just a story, right? Don't you remember in Year 1 we were all guessing about where it came from, and Charlie T told us that story – it just stuck. We don't even know the lady's name; we only call her Mrs Chestnut because it's a chestnut tree."

"Really?" said Grace, deflated. She'd forgotten that it was only Charlie T's story; she thought that was really what had happened. She'd told her sister about it and everything.

"Don't look so crest-fallen, Grace," said Mrs Jupiter, "I think it's a lovely story, and a very creative explanation of how the duck came to be in the tree."

"Just not a very likely one!" giggled Sebi.

"Can you think of a better one?" Grace asked.

"Not really," Sebi admitted. "Not without more information, anyway. I'd just be guessing, and that's pretty pointless."

"Well, not always," said Mrs Jupiter, looking thoughtful.

"I mean, it's difficult with no information I admit, but sometimes your best guess is a good place to start when you're trying to solve a puzzle with some of the facts. Just the other night I got home and realised I didn't have my keys. I remembered taking my purse out of my bag at the shop, and thought that maybe my keys had fallen out at the same time. Sure enough, they had been handed in at the shop."

"But that's not really a guess," said Sebi, looking a little confused, "it's... well it's something different."

"It sounds like a guess to me – and a useful one!" It was Grace's turn to look thoughtful. "I wonder what would happen if we never guessed?"

Discussion plan

- Can anyone think of a time when a guess has been useful to them?
- Why might we say that Mrs Jupiter used "Maybe..." thinking to find her keys?
- Is there a difference between the children's guess about Mrs Chestnut's duck and Mrs Jupiter's guess about her lost keys?
- What do you think people mean when they talk about an informed or an educated guess?
- Do you need curiosity and imagination to make an informed guess, or just information?
- What could Mrs Jupiter mean when she says that "Sometimes your best guess is a good place to start when you are trying to solve a puzzle"? If the guess is the start, what comes next?
- Guesses, even informed ones, often turn out to be wrong (Mrs Jupiter's keys might not have been at the shop, for example). Does that mean that we shouldn't make them?
- Should scientists ever make guesses (use "Maybe..." thinking) when they try to come up with explanations about the world? If so, what kind of guesses could be useful?

5

Tala's sunflower

Notes for the curious teacher

In the last lesson, we saw how scientists use **abductive reasoning** (or "Maybe…" thinking) to create a hypothesis. In this lesson, we'll see how **deductive reasoning** (or "If… then…" thinking) is used to put hypotheses to the test.

What is deductive reasoning?

Let's start with a simple example of deductive reasoning:

Tom says, "All men are mortal."
Zahra says, "Albert Einstein is a man."

Together, they conclude that, "***If*** all men are mortal, and Albert Einstein is a man, ***then*** Albert Einstein is mortal."

DOI: 10.4324/9781003663454-6

Tom begins with a general statement (a premise), and Zahra adds a more specific one. A *premise* is simply a statement from which another can be inferred. If both premises are true, then the conclusion **must** also be true. There is no way that all men can be mortal and any one man — Einstein included — can be immortal. Deductive reasoning guarantees true conclusions as long as the premises are correct.

How is deductive reasoning used in science?

Let's take a look at a famous example. In 1915, the aforementioned Albert Einstein hypothesised that massive objects curve, or "warp," space itself. This was hard for many people to believe — but, like all good scientific hypotheses, it could be tested empirically.

A little "If… then…" thinking led to a testable prediction:

If *massive objects curve space (premise 1),*
and the sun is a massive object (premise 2),
then *light from distant stars should appear bent as it passes near the sun.*

In 1919, a total solar eclipse presented an opportunity to measure any such bending of the light and to compare this measurement with predictions made using Einstein's equations. British astronomers, led by Arthur Eddington and Frank Watson Dyson, set out on expeditions to make the measurements — and they matched Einstein's predictions beautifully, making him a scientific celebrity!

Of course, one successful test doesn't prove a hypothesis for all time. We may have demonstrated that one massive object curves space and provided evidence to support Einstein's theory, but does that mean that we can reliably infer that they all will? How many massive objects would we need to test before we could be confident that we had discovered a general rule? Can we ever be confident that we won't find an exception?

That's the problem scientists face when they want to move from testing a hypothesis to establishing a law or principle — a topic we'll return to in the next lesson.

From the cosmos to the classroom

In the last lesson, we saw that apples float on water, but grapes sink. That led us, by abductive reasoning, to the hypothesis:

Maybe *apples float because they are light for their size.*

Scientists use the word *density* to describe how much mass an object has for its size. So, we might refine our idea to:

Maybe apples float because they are less dense than water.

Now we can use "If… then…" thinking to test our hypothesis:

If *apples float because they are less dense than water (premise 1),*
and lemons are less dense than water (premise 2),
then *lemons must float.*

If premises 1 and 2 are correct — as they are — then the conclusion must be true — and it is! Our hypothesis has passed its first test.

It's worth noting that in everyday language (as opposed to the language of formal logic), the two premises are often rolled into one. So we might more commonly say:

If *apples float because they are less dense than water,* ***then*** *lemons should float.*

Here, the specific premise that "lemons are less dense than water" is **assumed** as a kind of background knowledge. This is a more natural form of expression, but it's useful to be aware that the second premise is there — just hidden. If, to our surprise, an object sank, this could be because our hypothesis — that apples float because they are less dense than water — is wrong. But we shouldn't rush to reject it until we have checked our assumption about this particular object being less dense than water — it could be that this hidden premise is responsible for the surprising observation.

Why is this important?

Remember, one thing that distinguishes a *scientific* hypothesis is that it can be **tested empirically** and potentially shown to be wrong. Others, often based on belief or opinion, cannot be tested in this way. They are often said to be unscientific. This doesn't mean that they have no value, just that they aren't supported by empirical evidence.

The scientific community routinely uses "If… then…" thinking to test ideas and reject those that are not supported by evidence. This is a cornerstone of science – even if, in rare cases, testing must wait until better tools are available.

This kind of thinking also helps to protect us from **misinformation**. Conspiracy theories and fake news sometimes tell a simple and dramatic story. But if we pause and ask a single question —

*"**If** this is true, **then** what else must be true?"*

— many claims quickly fall apart. For example, faced with a claim that the Earth is flat, we might think:

If *the Earth is flat,* ***then*** *ships sailing into the distance would never fully disappear — they would just seem smaller.*

In fact, as ships sail away from us, they **do** disappear, hull first, over the horizon. The conclusion of our "If… then…" thinking is false, suggesting that the premise is also false — the Earth cannot be flat![1]

So deductive reasoning not only helps scientists make discoveries — it also helps all of us check everyday claims before we believe them.

In this lesson, the children will have opportunities to practise using "If… then…" thinking in both everyday and scientific contexts. They will also be challenged to identify non-scientific hypotheses — those that can't be tested. It's really up to you whether you want to introduce the language of deductive reasoning – "If… then…" thinking is fine for now.

Questions for reflection

- Can you recall a time when you have used deductive reasoning — "If… then…" thinking — to test an everyday hypothesis? Can you think of an everyday hypothesis that isn't testable in this way?
- What does this reveal about what makes a hypothesis testable?
- Can you think of any examples of potential misinformation that could be tested this way? Are there examples that the children in your class might encounter?
- If you give children opportunities to create hypotheses for surprising observations, they may come up with suggestions like these:
    - Metals feel colder than plastics because metals take longer to get warm. (Incorrect)
    - Some solids dissolve in water because the water breaks them up into tiny bits that you can't see. (Correct)

  - Plants grow towards the light because it's warmer in the light. (Incorrect)
    Choose one of these hypotheses. What "If… then…" statements might the children come up with to test it? What observations would confirm it? What observations would challenge it?
- How might giving children time to turn their explanations into testable "If… then…" predictions strengthen their understanding of scientific inquiry?

Lesson 5

Notes for the busy teacher

Learning aim: I can use "If… then…" thinking to test a hypothesis

This lesson introduces the use of deductive reasoning to test a hypothesis. Having arrived at a "best guess" through abductive reasoning, scientists can use the hypothesis to make predictions about what should happen ***if*** the hypothesis is correct. We can refer to this as "If… then…" thinking. It's important that hypotheses are tested so that we know whether we can rely on them to make accurate predictions. The more predictions are made and found to be correct, the more credible the hypothesis becomes. Even then, the hypothesis is not proven – there is always a possibility that it will fail a future test. Generally (though not always), scientific hypotheses can be tested through observable evidence and deduction. Others, often based in belief or opinion, cannot be tested in this way. These are often described as unscientific; this does not mean that they lack value, just that they are not supported by empirical evidence.

Session plan

Skills building exercise (warm-up)

Remind the pupils of their ground rules and the skills they have practised in previous lessons. An important part of thinking together is a willingness to challenge and test ideas to see if they are strong, or right. One way of doing that is to use "If… then…" thinking. This helps us to make predictions about what should happen ***if*** the idea is right – and then we can test our predictions.

- Place the pupils in groups of 3 and show them the image on Slide 2.
- Can the pupils finish Molly's sentence to show how the idea could be tested? Give the groups some time to think together before sharing a few ideas. They might say, "***If*** wearing a pink hat makes you good at spelling, ***then*** people who wear pink hats should get higher scores on spelling tests than people who don't."
- If desired, repeat the process for Slides 3 and 4. Pupils might suggest, "***If*** knock-knock jokes are the funniest, ***then*** people should laugh louder at them than at other jokes," and "***If*** the moon is made of cheese, ***then*** samples of the moon that have been brought back to Earth should be cheese!"

- Spend a little time reflecting on how "If… then…" thinking might be useful for testing suggestions in school and in life more generally.

Stimulus and discussion

- Read Tala's Sunflower to or with the class.
- Discuss the story with the children, making use of the discussion plan provided as appropriate. Do the pupils have questions in response to the story? These could be addressed now or collected and addressed following the main activity.

Main exercise

Scientists often use "If… then…" thinking to test hypotheses.

- Show the pupils Slide 9 and invite some children to read out the text.
- Give them time to think together in their 3's to construct an "If… then…" sentence that offers a testable prediction about the idea of light bulbs sharing power. An example might be, "***If*** the lamps are sharing power, ***then*** adding a third lamp should make them dimmer still".
- Invite some groups to share ideas. You could record the predictions and encourage the children to evaluate their usefulness.
- If desired, the predictions could be tested experimentally. (You could then set up a parallel circuit and ask the children for a prediction – "***If*** I add another bulb, ***then***…." This will demonstrate that hypotheses often need to be refined.)

- You could continue to step the pupils through the exercise using the slides, or you could use the worksheet provided to allow the pupils to work independently. There is no need to use all of the examples – some could lead to interesting investigations.
- Remind pupils to be guided by their ground rules as they think together.

Whole-class plenary

Slide 14 makes an important connection between scientific thinking and everyday life as it moves towards the testing of fake news or conspiracy theories.

- Show Slide 14 and ask the pupils to complete Bertie's sentence. Can they come up with statements such as, "***If*** the Earth is flat, ***then*** photographs from space should show a flat Earth/ships shouldn't slowly disappear over the horizon"?
- Ask them if "If… then…" thinking could protect them from fake news. Can they think of examples that could be tested?
- You could also show Slide 15, which includes some non-scientific hypotheses.
- Could these hypotheses be tested with "If… then…" thinking? Allow the children some time to think together and offer responses.
- These cases are problematic. For example, how do we define and measure "good things"? Is there an empirical way to show that dreams are or are not messages

from other planets? Can we know whether the barking dog is feeling love?

- People often say that these hypotheses are not scientific, because they cannot be tested with reason and observation. What do the children think about that?
- Finally, ask the children to look out for one idea they could test this week using "If… then…" thinking.

Metacognition

Give the groups of three time to think together around the following questions:

- How well did we use "If… then…" thinking to test ideas today? How could it help us think better together in future? Are there other ways to challenge and test ideas?
- Which other rules did the groups do well with? Why were they useful?
- Are there rules they need to focus on more next time? How will they help?

Resources

- Slide set to support the session
- Pupil worksheet to support independent group work if desired
- Practical equipment if you decide to test any of the predictions made

Talk prompts and vocabulary

Talk prompts

For this lesson's thinking together and working scientifically foci: "If… then…"

Vocabulary

Hypothesis: a proposed explanation made on the basis of limited evidence as a starting point for further investigation, **or, for children**, a "maybe" idea that explains what you notice and can be tested to see if it might be true.

Deductive reasoning: a logical process of moving from general ideas or premises to a specific conclusion, **or, for children**, using "If… then…" thinking to see what must happen or must be true if your idea is correct. (No need to use the term "deductive reasoning" with the children if you prefer not to.)

Premise: a statement you start with when using deductive reasoning. If the premises are true, the conclusion must be true too. (Example: Premise – "All cats have tails.") (Again, no need to use this term with the children.)

Prediction: a statement about what you expect to observe if your hypothesis is correct. A prediction applies deductive reasoning to a hypothesis, but the prediction itself is what you then test. (Example: "If I drop a lemon in water, then it will float.")

Stimulus: Tala's sunflower

It was the end of the school day, and Tala couldn't help but beam with pride. Her classroom plant, a little sunflower sprout, was now the tallest in the room. Mr Robins had even given it a special spot by the window.

"Tala, how come your sunflower is growing so fast?" asked Karl, staring at his own, much smaller plant.

Tala shrugged, but then she had an idea. "I talk to it every day," she said. "Maybe that's why."

Karl looked curious. "You talk to your plant? What do you say?"

"Just stuff like 'Good morning!' or 'You're doing great, keep growing!' It's as if it likes the encouragement, or the sound."

Karl frowned. "That sounds like a fun idea, but does it really make plants grow? Plants don't have ears!"

Mr Robins, who had been listening with interest, smiled. "Tala has made an interesting hypothesis! She thinks that talking to her plant is what makes it grow faster. Now, how can we test this out with a bit of 'If… then…' thinking?"

Grace looked puzzled. "What's 'If… then…' thinking?"

"Sorry, Grace," said Mr Robins,

"I just mean that if Tala's guess is right, then we should be able to use it to figure out what else will happen and check to see if it does. So, if talking to plants makes them grow faster…."

"Then… talking to the other little sprouts should make them grow faster too!" exclaimed Grace.

"Brilliant!" said Mr Robins. "And if we don't talk to some of the plants, then they shouldn't grow as fast."

Karl was getting excited now. "Let's divide the plants into two groups. We'll talk to one group every day and really encourage them, and we'll leave the other group alone. If Grace is right, then the ones we talk to will grow faster."

A week later, it was time to reveal the results! The children had carefully measured the heights of all the sunflower sprouts; Tala felt sure that those that had been given plenty of encouragement would be the champions! "Well, Mr Robins," she said, "What's the verdict?"

"Hmm," Mr Robins began, "Some of the ones we talked to grew a little more, but the difference isn't that big. And a couple of the ones we didn't talk to grew well too."

"Does that mean my idea was wrong?" asked Tala, feeling disappointed.

"Not necessarily, Tala. It just means that the evidence we have so far doesn't support it."

Seeing Tala's disappointment, Mr Robins went on in a kind voice, "Sometimes, even good guesses don't turn out to be true. But knowing what's not true is one step closer to finding out what is true!"

Tala smiled a little. "So maybe something else is helping my plant grow?"

"Maybe," said Karl, "like all that sunshine it gets by the window!"

"So, if we put all the sunflowers in the window, then they should start growing faster!", yelled Grace.

"This is fun," said Tala, "Can all guesses be tested with 'If… then…' thinking?"

Discussion plan

- Can you remember what a hypothesis is? What was Tala's hypothesis?
- Do you think it was a good hypothesis? Why/why not?
- What did Mr Robins mean by "If… then…" thinking? Can you find examples of it in the story?
- Have you ever used "If… then…" thinking to test out a guess? Can you think of any examples?
- Tala's hypothesis didn't seem to be right. Why might Mr Robins have said that "the evidence we have so far doesn't seem to support it"? Is that just a kind way of saying it's wrong?
- What could Mr Robins have meant when he said that "…knowing what's not true is one step closer to finding out what is true!"?
- Tala asked if all guesses can be tested by "If… then…" thinking. What do you think?
- Can we find examples of guesses or hypotheses that can't be tested in this way?

Note

1 More formally, this piece of reasoning might be set out as follows:

Premise 1: *On a flat surface, objects moving away do not disappear bottom-first — they only get smaller.*
Premise 2: *The Earth is flat.*
Conclusion: *Therefore, ships sailing away on Earth will not disappear bottom-first.*

In this case, the first premise — assumed in our informal expression — is easy to test and observe, so we doubt the second premise — that the Earth is flat.

6

The swan

Notes for the curious teacher

In previous lessons we've seen how abductive reasoning, or "Maybe..." thinking, can be used to create a hypothesis to explain an observation. We used examples like:

***Maybe** apples float because they are less dense than water.*

We've also seen that deductive reasoning or "If... then..." thinking can be used to test hypotheses:

***If** apples float because they are less dense than water, **then** lemons should float too.*

Now we turn our attention to a third form of reasoning used by scientists to infer general rules from a limited number of

DOI: 10.4324/9781003663454-7

examples. It's called **inductive reasoning**, or **"So the rule is…" thinking**. Scientists find it incredibly useful, though, as we'll see, some people have used it to call the authority of science into question.

What is inductive reasoning?

Here's a simple example:

On Monday, you notice that the grass is wet when you get up.
On Tuesday, the grass is wet again when you get up.
On Wednesday, you see the same thing — wet grass when you get up.

You might think:

***So the rule is**: the grass is always wet in the morning.*

That's **inductive reasoning** – you're looking at a series of observations, noticing a pattern, and suggesting a general rule. It's different from **abductive reasoning**, which offers a possible explanation for an observation. If, on Monday morning, you had said:

***Maybe** the grass is wet because it rained in the night.*

then you would have been reasoning abductively. Inductive reasoning takes us from a set of examples to a suggested general rule. Abductive reasoning takes us from an observation to the most likely explanation.

How is inductive reasoning used in science?

Let's return to the floating fruits. Having found that lemons do indeed float, our hypothesis that apples might float because they are less dense than water begins to seem more likely. So we might try a number of other objects that are less dense than water and find that they float too. This might lead us to suggest:

***So the rule is**: all objects that are less dense than water float.*

Inductive reasoning has allowed us to suggest a general rule. Creating general rules by spotting patterns in a number of consistent observations is a cornerstone of scientific progress because:

- **It makes predictions possible**. A well-tested rule can be applied to new situations, allowing scientists (and engineers, doctors, etc.) to anticipate what will happen. For example, if the rule "metals expand when heated" is consistently found to be true, we can predict how railway tracks, bridges, or machinery will behave in heatwaves.
- **It organises knowledge**. Instead of remembering hundreds of separate facts, a single principle can explain many different cases. For example, if the rule "objects fall towards the Earth because of gravity" is consistently true, we can use it to explain apples falling, balls rolling downhill, and satellites orbiting.
- **It allows testing and refinement**. A clearly stated rule can be checked against fresh data, either strengthening confidence in it or showing where it needs to change.
- **It helps ideas travel**. Once expressed as a rule, the knowledge can be shared and used by others to solve different problems.

Of course, it's not just scientists who rely on inductive reasoning. If the 07:40 bus gets you to work on time for five days in a row, you might reasonably think:

***So the rule is**: if I catch the 07:40 I'll be in on time!*

Having experienced several loaves of bread becoming stale after leaving them on top of the breadbin, you could usefully conclude:

So the rule is: *bread goes stale if it's left out in the open.*

In truth, it would be hard for us to function without using inductive reasoning to make predictions about the future.

The problem of induction

Scientific rules are strong, useful and testable – but are they certain? Back to our floating and sinking experiments. Just how much confidence should we have in our new rule:

So the rule is: *all objects less dense than water float?*

You might agree that such a conclusion would be premature based on just a handful of observations! So how many objects would we need to test: 10? 100? 1000? Even if we have tested 10,000 objects that are less dense than water and found that all of them float, can we be *certain* that the next one will float as well?

This question poses a challenge to science that was most famously articulated by the Scottish philosopher David Hume in the eighteenth century. Hume believed that there is no logical reason for assuming that the future will resemble the past. In deductive reasoning, true premises lead with certainty to a true conclusion – ***if*** all men are mortal and Einstein is a man, ***then*** Einstein is most certainly mortal. This isn't the case with inductive reasoning – if apples float and lemons float then it does not follow with any certainty that other low-density objects will float too.

Inductive reasoning – and, by extension, much of scientific knowledge – deals in probabilities rather than certainties. If a rule has been followed a large number of times, then it can be said to have a great deal of corroborating evidence and can be relied upon with confidence. We can reasonably say that it is **probable** that it will be followed again – but we can't claim that it's certain.

This is an important point. Scientific rules or laws help us to make reliable predictions and to organise our thinking about the universe – but they are **fallible**. So the scientific community has to retain a good degree of humility – of openness to the possibility they are wrong. In fact, it's by testing laws to breaking point and sometimes disproving them that science is able to make progress.

That seems like a healthy attitude for scientists, and a healthy attitude for all of us to have. We can believe with confidence that the next apple we let go of will fall to Earth, but we can't be certain. In the same way, we can believe that the 07:40 bus will get us to work on time, but we have to live with the possibility that it won't, and that investment account that has performed well for years may well deliver good returns – but it might not. It's essential to hold beliefs based on good evidence that help us navigate life. At the same time, we should remain open to the possibility that we might be wrong.

In this lesson, children will have the opportunity to practise using "So the rule is…" thinking in both everyday and scientific contexts. They are also introduced to the notion that apparent "rules" can be broken and are led to think together about how they might respond when this happens.

Now, raise your hand if you agree that:

***The rule is**: all swans are white!*

Questions for reflection

- Where do you use "So the rule is..." thinking in everyday life? What pattern did you notice, and how many times did it need to happen before you felt confident in your rule?
- How reliable is your rule? Does it always hold true, or only usually? How many exceptions would it take before you started to question, modify or abandon it?
- How might it feel if you have to modify or abandon the rule? Does that mean you were wrong or unwise to follow it in the first place? What does this tell us about how we learn from experience and how we cope with uncertainty?
- Is a broken rule a failure, or simply a part of the way that knowledge grows?
- Imagine the children in your class suggest a hypothesis: "***Maybe*** metals are better conductors of heat than plastics." They test it: "***If*** metals are better conductors of heat than plastics, ***then*** if we heat these rods at one end the metal ones should heat up faster at the other end" – and their prediction is correct. How could you help them to practise and to recognise the value of "So the rule is..." thinking?
- What do you think about the idea that general rules should be seen as tools for thinking, not cages that restrict thinking?
- How could you support the children in your class to recognise the limitations of forming general rules on the basis of limited examples and the importance of remaining open to exceptions?

Lesson 6

Notes for the busy teacher

Learning aim: I can use "So the rule is..." thinking to make useful rules and predictions

This session introduces children to a third type of reasoning: inductive reasoning. Inductive reasoning takes patterns found by observing a relatively limited sample and treats them as general. Here we call it, "So the rule is..." thinking. It leads to conclusions which **may** be false, despite the premises being true. The black swan is a classic example – if you have only ever seen white swans it would seem reasonable to conclude that all swans might be (but are not certain to be) white. Inductive reasoning helps us (and scientists) to spot patterns and suggest **general rules**. For example, if you observe that ten different kinds of fruit rot faster at room temperature than in a refrigerator, you might use inductive reasoning to form a general rule such as "fruits rot faster at room temperature than when refrigerated." This rule, and others like it, are not certain to be true; exceptions may, one day, be found. It takes only one exception to disprove a rule! Knowledge based on inductive reasoning (which covers much scientific knowledge) is based on probabilities rather than certainties. This is an important message, because many people expect scientists to give them certainty about the world, or misrepresent them as always thinking that they have the right answer. In fact, scientists need the **humility** to understand that their rules (or laws), predictions, hypotheses, and theories may not be correct. Indeed, finding an exception to a pattern or rule can be an exciting moment in science, because it drives us on to understand more.

Session plan

Skills building exercise (warm-up)

Remind the pupils of their rules and of the skills they have practised. Another important skill is being able to say why you think what you think. In this exercise, the pupils should use the word "**because**" to introduce reasons for their ideas. They should, of course, continue to follow their ground rules and apply the other skills they have practised.

- Place the pupils in groups of three and show the first part of Slide 2. Molli-with-an-i likes Cheddar cheese, but not milk. What might the pattern be? Give a short time for groups to make suggestions, making sure they share their reasons.
- Show Molli's second like – custard. This time, give pupils some time to think together about a possible pattern.
- Repeat with Molli's third like, by which time the pupils may well agree that Molli seems to like yellow food! Can they be certain that she only likes yellow

food? How many of Molli's favourite foods would they need to find out about before they were certain?

- Repeat the exercise with Slides 3 and 4. Be sure to ask the pupils whether they can be sure that Molli only likes water or games with round balls. Maintain a focus on giving reasons.

Stimulus and discussion

- Read The Swan to the class.
- Discuss the story with the children, making use of the discussion plan provided as appropriate. Do the pupils have questions in response to the story? These could be addressed now or collected and addressed following the main activity.

Main exercise

- Show the first line on Slide 9 ("Copper conducts electricity..."). Scientists often look for patterns and make rules in much the same way as the pupils did during the warm-up exercise, and Sebi did in the story. What pattern might emerge on this slide?
- Work through the slide as you did with Slides 2–4.
- It's important that children don't leave with the misconception that only metals conduct electricity – make sure you address the "broken rules" on the final slide.
- You could continue to step the pupils through the exercise using the slides, or you could use the worksheet provided to allow the pupils to think together in

groups of three. Remind them of their talk rules, and of the emphasis on giving reasons.

- The slides could be used in a plenary if desired (Answers – the rules are: metals are conductors of electricity, non-metals are not; mammals are warm-blooded or endothermic, reptiles are not; migrating birds fly to warmer places for the winter; features that you get from the environment are not inherited; this spring stretches by 5 cm every time 100 g is added. With a little bit of "If…then…" thinking (deductive reasoning) the children might predict that the spring will stretch to 30 cm with the addition of another 100 g; Halley's comet is seen every 75 or 76 years. With a little bit of "If…then…" thinking (deductive reasoning) the children might predict that the comet is next expected in 2061).

Whole-class plenary

Show the final slide. As the pupils can see, rules made in this way can be broken. Invite them to discuss Molli's and Tala's questions in their groups. Patterns and rules like the ones made today can really help us to understand the world around us and to make useful predictions, but we have to remember that they could be wrong. Some scientific rules (such as objects always falling to the centre of the Earth) have stood the test of time and are relied upon with very high confidence, but even these remain open to testing. It's important for scientists – and for all of us – to be open to the possibility of being wrong.

Metacognition

Give the groups of three time to think together around the following questions:

- Did everyone give reasons for their ideas today? How does this help to increase the quality of thinking together?
- Which other rules did the groups do well with? Why were they useful?
- Are there rules they need to focus on more next time? How will they help?

Resources

- Slide set to support the session
- Pupil worksheet to support independent group work if desired
- A small bag filled with objects of the same type (e.g. 1p coins, blue blocks). (optional)

Talk prompts and vocabulary

Talk prompts

For this lesson's thinking together focus: "I think… because"; "Why do you think…?"

For this lesson's thinking scientifically focus: "So the rule is…"

Vocabulary

Inductive reasoning: a method of drawing conclusions by going from the specific to the general **or, for children**, using "So the rule is..." thinking to suggest rules from the patterns in the things you see. (No need to use the term inductive reasoning with the children if you would prefer not to – "So the rule is…" thinking is fine for now.)

Likely: probably true or probably will happen.

Certain: definitely true or will definitely happen.

Generalise: make a general rule based on a limited number of specific examples, **or, for children**, to make a rule based on a few examples you have seen.

Stimulus: The swan

Newton Primary was right next to the town park, and Galileo class was particularly lucky because they had a great view of the lake with its famous white swans. Sebi loved watching them (although he sometimes got a bit distracted from what Mr Robins was saying). He also walked through the park every day on his way to and from school, and he often stopped to watch them, their white feathers gleaming in the reflection from the water.

That day the class was doing work on similes. Sebi looked down at his worksheet. The first one was "As blue as…." Sebi thought for a moment and then wrote "the sky." Then he stopped. No, the sky wasn't always blue, sometimes it was grey or white with cloud. Early in the morning or in the evening it could be pink or orange or red. So he kept on writing, "As blue as the sky on a sunny afternoon."

He looked at the next one. "As yellow as…". "Hmm, maybe cheese," he thought. But then he remembered that his mum ate that weird stuff that was white with blue and green mould, so cheese isn't always yellow. "As yellow as… a daffodil petal," he wrote in the end.

Next on the sheet was "As white as…." Well, he thought, at least this one was easy. He gazed out of the window at the swans gliding across the lake. "As white as… a swan," he wrote, and looked out of the window at the swans again. At that moment he noticed something very, very strange on the lake. He stared in shock and pressed his nose against the window: it was a swan, but it wasn't white, it was black. "Swans are white," he thought. "What on earth is happening? Every swan I've ever seen is white, so how come that one is black?"

"Is everything all right, Sebi?" called Mr Robins loudly.

"Err – well, not really, Mr Robins," Sebi replied, sadly. He explained his mistake.

"Ah," mused Mr Robins, "So you thought something like 'All the swans I have ever seen are white, so all the swans in the world must be white.'"

"Yes. It sounds a bit silly when you say it like that." Sebi felt embarrassed.

"Not at all!" Mr Robins exclaimed. "We all have to use our experiences to make predictions about things we haven't experienced yet. How would we manage if we didn't?"

"What do you mean?" asked Sebi.

Mr Robins thought for a moment. "Well, what time did you and your mum leave the house to drive to school this morning?"

"Twenty past eight."

"And were you here on time?"

"Yes, we arrived at 8:45, and that's a nice time to meet everyone in the yard. It's the same every morning."

"So, when do you need to leave the house to get here on time tomorrow?"

"Well, twenty past eight, I suppose."

"You see!" said Mr Robins, "You are using your experiences to make a useful prediction – we have to do that sort of thing all the time."

"So, now I'm saying 'Every time I left the house at twenty-past eight, I got to school on time, so I will always get to school on time if I leave at twenty-past eight.' But the swan thing went wrong…" Sebi looked worried, "…so this could go wrong too!"

Molli-with-an-i had been listening carefully to all this. "Mmm – so can we ever be certain about things that haven't happened yet?" she asked.

Discussion plan

- Was Sebi silly to think that all swans are white?
- What if he had only ever seen two swans, and both were white? Would he be silly to believe that all swans are white?
- How many swans would he need to see before it would be OK for him to believe that all swans are white?
- Could he ever be *certain* that all swans are white?
- If you want to give the children another example of predictions from patterns, use a small bag filled with objects of the same type (e.g. 1p coins, blue blocks). Pull one out of the bag. Can they make a prediction about what else is in the bag?

Pull out another one. Can they make a prediction now? How sure are they? Keep going four or five times. Then ask them to make up a rule about the objects in the bag, for example, all of the coins in the bag are 1p coins. How certain can they be?

- Do you ever use this kind of "So the rule is…" thinking like Sebi uses to get to school on time? Is it useful? Does it go wrong sometimes (can the rules be broken)?
- If you'd been testing objects to see if they float or sink, you might have spotted a pattern and decided:

  So the rules is: all objects that are lighter for their size than water float.

  How many objects would you need to test before you would have proven that the rule is true? Five? Fifty? Five hundred? Five million?

- Can scientists say, "Every object we have seen fall on Earth, falls towards the centre of the Earth, ***so the rule is***: all objects fall towards the centre of the Earth"? Could they be certain of this? Would it be better to say that it's **likely** that all objects fall towards the centre of the Earth?

7

Wonky sheep

Notes for the curious teacher

So far, we've seen that science is based on observation, measurement, and experiment – it's empirical. We've also seen that it's rational, which, among other things, means that it makes use of various well-established forms of reasoning – abductive ("Maybe…") to create a hypothesis, deductive ("If… then…") to test the hypothesis, and inductive ("So the rule is…") to suggest a general rule.

As a scientist, being rational includes making judgements about whether a change of direction is needed: what is the evidence really telling me about this hypothesis? How much weight should I give to this evidence? Are my personal biases leading me to behave in an irrational way? Failure to ask

DOI: 10.4324/9781003663454-8

questions like these could lead us to move from a hypothesis through to a generalised rule with undue haste.

In this lesson, we introduce a fourth kind of thinking: sceptical thinking, or "Hang on a minute..." thinking. This involves a pause to question the claim that's being made and the evidence on which it's based. It stops us from jumping to conclusions too quickly, and it helps us to tell the difference between a good explanation and a mistake, or even bad science. It's not always easy for an individual, so it's important that the scientific community as a whole adopts a sceptical stance towards new claims.

What is sceptical thinking?

In 1917, nine-year-old Frances Griffiths and 16-year-old Elsie Wright photographed fairies in their garden. Three years later, the photos came to the attention of Sir Arthur Conan Doyle, the celebrated author of the Sherlock Holmes stories, and he published them. He did have doubts and even asked experts to examine the photos to see if they were fakes. But, somewhere inside, he wanted them to be real because they supported his ideas about the supernatural.

He wasn't alone. As the images spread around the world, many thousands of people believed them too. It wasn't until 1983 that Frances and Elsie admitted that the fairies were made out of paper! Frances said, "I can't understand to this day why people were taken in. They wanted to be taken in."

I guess we've all been there – I'm sure you can think of an April Fool prank or a practical joke that took you in – hook, line, and sinker! Maybe it's partly because we want these things to be real that we suspend our critical faculties – we fail to ask questions like: is there good evidence for this? Who wants me to believe this and why? If this were true, what else would have to be true?

If we adopt a sceptical stance (get into the habit of saying, "Hang on a minute..."), we consciously maintain a questioning and doubtful attitude towards claims rather than accepting them immediately. That's not to say that we refuse to believe anything – but we do suspend belief until we are satisfied that it's based on good evidence. Of course, we can't check everything ourselves, so we need to develop good judgement about who we can reasonably trust. The sceptical stance adopted by the scientific community as a whole is one reason for trusting in science.

Sceptical thinking and the scientific community

Let's look at two famous examples of the need for scientific scepticism.

In 2011, scientists working at Gran Sasso in Italy published an extraordinary experimental finding. They had measured tiny, subatomic particles (neutrinos) travelling faster than the speed of light. What's so extraordinary about that? Well, it contradicts Einstein's theory of special relativity which tells us that nothing can travel faster than the speed of light. This is one of those theories that started out as a piece of "Maybe..." thinking, withstood the test of "If... then... thinking," and became an accepted rule. In fact, it became a cornerstone of our understanding of the universe.

So, was this a moment when science needed a radical change of direction? The scientific community was sceptical – as, to be fair, were the scientists involved in the discovery. It's not that they weren't open to the possibility of the observation being true, but they adhered to the maxim, "Extraordinary claims require extraordinary evidence." A few months after the publication of the original claim, and after a lot of scrutiny and attempts to replicate the result, it was found that a faulty cable connection had led to false results. Einstein's theory was safe – at least for the time being!

This shows scientists themselves welcoming scrutiny of their results, rather than trying to defend them at all costs. The sceptical stance taken by the scientific community – the willingness to work in collaboration to check and re-check the claims made – prevented a momentous wrong-turn for science. A nice example of, "Hang on a minute..." thinking!

Now let's look at another example, this time of bad science that caused lasting harm. In 1998, British scientist Andrew Wakefield published an article suggesting that a vaccine given to prevent measles, mumps, and rubella – the MMR vaccine – could cause autism in children. Over time, a sceptical scientific community showed that Wakefield's results were based on a tiny sample – just 12 children – and on uncontrolled, unethical procedures. Much larger, more rigorous studies found no evidence of a link between the MMR vaccine and autism. In 2010, Wakefield was struck off the UK medical register for "serious professional misconduct" including the falsification of evidence in his original publication, which was retracted. The scientific community was clear in communicating that the results could not be trusted.

Sadly, some media professionals did not adopt a sceptical attitude, and the story of the link between MMR and autism spread widely. This has caused a great deal of distress to parents and led to falling vaccination rates, exposing children to serious illness. The absence of a sceptical stance in the media and in some members of the medical profession caused lasting harm.

We can see, then, that it's not just scientists who need to be able to take a sceptical stance. In a world in which misinformation is everywhere, all of us, including our children, need to learn to "hang on a minute" and ask those critical questions: is there good evidence for this? Who wants me to believe this and why? If this were true, what else would have to be true?

Of course, there's a balance to be struck here. If we began to feel that we couldn't trust anyone or believe anything, life would become extremely difficult. That's why we need to know who we can trust and why we can trust them. We trust a doctor more than a stranger on social media because we understand that the doctor has been well-trained and works within a framework of regulation and oversight. And we can have trust in science because we know that individual scientists work within a collaborative and sceptical community that corrects itself.

Ultimately, we each have some responsibility to take a sceptical stance that can protect us from unwarranted claims, unscrupulous advertising, and untrustworthy news. In this lesson, children are shown a series of claims that seem "scientific" – but not all of them are based on good evidence! They have the chance to think together to develop some "sceptical questions" with which to interrogate the claims, and to reflect on how the scientific community adopts a sceptical stance to prevent the spread of "bad science."

Hopefully, the chosen examples will help children to make a connection between scientific – in this case, sceptical – thinking and the ways it can help them to protect themselves from potentially harmful "fake news."

Questions for reflection

- Can you recall a time when you were taken in by misinformation – perhaps a practical joke, a scam, or an unscrupulous advertisement? What critical questions could a little "Hang on a minute…" thinking have helped you to ask?

- How can you cultivate a sceptical mindset while retaining an openness to new and sometimes surprising learning?
- How does the scientific community balance openness to radical new ideas with the need for rigorous scepticism? To what extent does this help to justify public trust in science?
- In science lessons, do children feel free to challenge ideas – including yours? What classroom norms make that possible, and what norms might stand in the way?
- What role does collaborative group work play in helping pupils take a sceptical stance? How might working with others protect them from being misled – or help them to notice flaws in their own reasoning?
- Could lessons about scepticism protect children from misinformation? Could there be unintended consequences?

Lesson 7

Notes for the busy teacher

Learning aim: I can use "Hang on a minute..." thinking to help me decide if something is true or not

This session encourages children to think about how to question what they've been told – to take a sceptical stance towards questionable information. The idea of trustworthy evidence is introduced. The scientific community takes what might be described as a sceptical stance towards claims made by its own members. As we've already seen, scientists don't accept hypotheses at face value – they test them (often with "If.. then..." thinking), looking out for evidence that they're not true. They try to replicate each other's results and check each other's methods. There's an important message here, further developed in the next lesson, about why we might trust the scientific community. In a digital age, where children will be presented with an abundance of information that they are not able to check through experiment, developing strategies to question what they read and hear is important. Adopting a sceptical stance, or using "Hang on a minute..." thinking, might help us avoid falling for stories like the one about the wonky sheep!

Session plan

Skills building exercise (warm-up)

- Remind the pupils of their rules and of the skills they have practised. Today they will explore another way of respectfully challenging ideas or claims: asking questions. In this exercise, the pupils should try to think of questions to put ideas to the test.
- Tell the class you're going to play "Two truths and a lie." Give them three statements, two of which are true and one of which is a lie. They have to decide which is which. The statements should be personal to you (e.g. I have four cats, I never miss an episode of..., I once..., etc.). Have the statements on the board. You could also prepare these statements on paper to give to

each group so that they can write their sceptical questions underneath.

- Divide the class into groups of three. They have to come up with questions to ask about each of the statements to help them work out which is true and which is not. They should spend some time thinking about which questions would be good (e.g. What are the names of your cats?). You could also give the children question stems to help them (i.e. What…? When…? Where…? Why…? How…?). Remind them to follow their ground rules as they seek to reach agreement about the best questions.
- Allow each group to ask you one of their questions. Can they spot the lie?

Stimulus and discussion

- Read Wonky Sheep to the class
- Discuss the story with the children, making use of the discussion plan provided as appropriate. Do the pupils have questions in response to the story? These could be addressed now or collected and addressed following the main activity.

Main exercise

- The slides provide three more suggestions for "Two truths and a lie" in a science context. You may only want to use one or two of these rather than all three, or you might want to give groups of pupils a choice of which one they focus on. You could, of course, create alternatives of your own.

- Place the pupils in groups of three and ask them to think together about which of the claims might be untrue.
- Remind them of Bertie's suggestion about saying "Hang on a minute..." and testing claims with questions and requests for evidence. What questions could they ask of the characters on the slide(s)? What evidence might they expect to see? How could the claims be investigated?
- Let the pupils think together about this and ask them to compile a list of suggestions.
- If there is time, and you have the necessary facilities, give the groups the opportunity to ask their questions in a web browser or an AI tool such as ChatGPT. Can they find sufficiently convincing answers/evidence to be sure about which statements are true or false? This could lead to a wider discussion about trustworthy websites, corroborating evidence, and so on.
- The untrue claims are: magnets in earrings and bracelets can help people to lose weight; the position of the sun at the time you are born can affect your behaviour; eating lots of grapefruit can help you to burn fat, use more energy, and so lose weight.

Whole-class plenary

Show the penultimate slide. Can the pupils suggest how scientists or the scientific community work together to spot false claims like these? In the case of the faster-than-light particles, the scientists involved found that faulty equipment had caused incorrect measurements. In the case of the cheap, safe nuclear energy, scientists around the world tried to copy the experiments that had been described, but no one could do it. Eventually, it was found that mistakes had been made in the original experiment and the results had not been interpreted properly.

So sceptical or "Hang on a minute..." thinking is what keeps science honest. It stops us from jumping to conclusions too quickly, and it helps us to tell the difference between a good explanation and a mistake or even bad science.

The final slide provides a summary of our "scientific thinking" toolkit. Can the children see how all four kinds of thinking are needed?

Metacognition

Give the groups of three time to think together around the following questions:

- Did everyone use "Hang on a minute..." thinking today? Were they able to ask questions to test the claims they saw?
- How did working together help you spot mistakes or weak ideas that you might have missed on your own?
- How can this use of questioning help to keep us safe?
- Respectfully challenging other people's ideas is one of the rules for thinking together. How does this help us to think things through well?
- Which other rules did the groups do well with? Why were they useful?
- Are there rules they need to focus on more next time? How will they help?

Resources

- Slide set to support the session
- Tablets/computers for each group and internet access

Talk prompts and vocabulary

Talk prompts

For this lesson's thinking together and working scientifically foci: "Hang on a minute…"; "What…?"; "When…?"; "Where…?"; "Why…?"; "How…?"; "What's the evidence for…?"

Vocabulary

Sceptical: not easily convinced; questioning.

Evidence: facts or information that are used to decide whether a belief or claim is true.

Scientific community: scientists from all over the world who work together, share ideas and results, and test each other's findings.

Stimulus: Wonky sheep

At break time, Mr Robins' class were doing what they usually did: eating snacks, playing football, and climbing on the adventure playground. But not Ama. She was standing by herself in a corner of the playground with her arms folded. Suddenly, she kicked the bench she was standing next to. Hard. She wished she hadn't, because it really hurt, but she was so cross.

Her attack on the innocent bench had caught the attention of some of the other children. "What's up, Ama?" asked Karl kindly.

"My sister," grumbled Ama. "She told me another one of her stories this morning. And as usual, I believed her. But she just made it up! And she laughed at me! I felt so silly."

"What was the story?" asked Bertie.

"She said that when sheep live where it's hilly, their legs on one side of their body grow longer so they can keep their balance on the hill."

Bertie thought about it. "Well, that kind of makes sense," he said. "I can see why you believed her."

"No it doesn't!" broke in Karl. "That would only work if the sheep always faced the same way. And what would happen if it ever came off of the hill? It'd be wonky!"

Ama wasn't in the mood. "I know, Karl!" she snapped. "But Bertie is right too. It did kind of make sense. And she just has this way of sounding so believable."

"Well, when she tells you something, just don't believe it," suggested Bertie.

"I can't do that!" answered Ama, "It's not like she always makes things up, and she knows way more than I do; even some things that sound silly to me could be true."

"And they could be lies," said Karl.

"Exactly," said Ama. "How can I know what's true and what's not?"

The bell rang, and Bertie and Karl walked back to their classroom with Ama. Bertie was lost in thought for a while, then he said, "You know, Ama, maybe you shouldn't believe or not believe the things she says — at least, not right away."

"Go on...," Ama encouraged him.

"Well, maybe you need to pause – to say 'Hang on a minute...' to yourself. Then you can test her – you know, ask her some questions, or ask for evidence."

"Mmm," Ama mused. "Do we always need evidence before we believe what someone says?"

Discussion plan

- Have you ever fallen for a story like the one about wonky sheep?
- Why do we believe such things sometimes?
- How can we protect ourselves from believing things that aren't true?
- What do you think about Bertie's suggestion that Ama should say "Hang on a minute..." and test her sister with questions?
- How could she do this respectfully? Why is it important to be respectful?
- What questions could Ama have asked about the wonky sheep?
- What does Bertie mean by "evidence"?
- Do we always need evidence before we believe someone?
- Is there a connection between the way Bertie wants Ama to think about the wonky sheep story and the way scientists think? What do scientists do when they have a hypothesis?
- Should we always believe what scientists tell us, or should we ask questions and look for evidence?

8

Dinosaurs

Notes for the curious teacher

In the last lesson, we explored the role of sceptical thinking (the "Hang on a minute…" mindset) in science and in life more generally. The sceptical stance taken by the scientific community – the willingness of scientists to engage in critical scrutiny of each other's work – was suggested to be a reason for trusting science.

In this lesson, we extend our thinking about why the scientific community might be seen as trustworthy. We'll do this by taking a look at the role of evidence and what constitutes good evidence, and by introducing the idea of peer review. We'll also draw out connections between a scientific approach to

 DOI: 10.4324/9781003663454-9

evidence and the role of evidence in protecting us from misinformation and fake news.

What do scientists mean by evidence?

The Cambridge Dictionary offers a definition of evidence as "anything that helps to prove that something is or is not true." In Chapter 3 we encountered the idea that one of the defining characteristics of science is that it is empirical. That means that the evidence that scientists rely on as they test the "truth" of their hypotheses and theories is gathered through their senses, often with the help of tools and instruments. They rely on observation, measurement, and experiment.

It's worth noticing, though, that what scientists actually collect are data — the raw observations or measurements. These only become evidence when they are interpreted in relation to a particular question. Let's look at an example:

Data. There is a puddle of water on the kitchen floor.
Evidence. Because the puddle is right in front of the fridge, this observation can be taken as evidence that the fridge might be leaking.
Hypothesis. From this evidence, we propose the idea that the fridge is leaking.

Notice how the **data** are just the "facts of the matter" – what anyone could observe. The **evidence** is that same data but now interpreted in relation to a question or context. The **hypothesis** is the explanatory idea we propose on the basis of the evidence.

Of course, the same puddle could also be interpreted as evidence for a different hypothesis ("the dog knocked over its water bowl"), which shows why evidence is always open to interpretation and debate. We rely on abductive reasoning ("Maybe..." thinking) to guide us towards a plausible, testable hypothesis.

What counts as good evidence?

Not all evidence carries equal weight. Scientists tend to evaluate evidence in terms of:

- **Reliability**. Was the data gathered carefully and can it be repeated?
- **Validity**. Does the evidence really show what it claims to?
- **Corroboration**. Is it supported by multiple, independent sources?
- **Coherence**. Does it fit well with the wider body of scientific knowledge?
- **Peer scrutiny**. Has it been checked and criticised by other scientists? (i.e. has there been peer review?)

This last point deserves further emphasis. Before scientists can publish new findings, other scientists in the same field examine the methods and conclusions to check for errors or bias. While the system is not perfect – mistakes still slip through, and reviewers can disagree – it provides an important safeguard against unchecked claims.

This connects back to the idea of the scientific community as self-correcting. Over time, weaker ideas fall away and stronger ones gain acceptance, because the evidence is repeatedly tested, questioned, and refined. Peer review is central to science's claim to trustworthiness.

Primary and secondary evidence

In science, primary evidence comes directly from observations or measurements (for example, a fossil, a crater, or a chemical analysis). But for most of us – and certainly for children – our knowledge of science relies on **secondary evidence**: the testimony of scientists and the reporting of their work. This is why *trust* matters so much. We can't all collect dinosaur fossils ourselves, but we can weigh up whether the testimony of palaeontologists, checked through peer review, is more reliable than the claims of a YouTuber.

Evidence in everyday life

Of course, it's not only scientists who engage with evidence. Children already use evidence in everyday decisions, even if they don't call it that. They rely on **primary evidence**: for example, when watching whether a football crossed the line, or checking whether a piece of homework is complete. They also rely on **secondary evidence**: for instance, when trusting what adults or doctors say about a healthy lifestyle, or when choosing a film to see based on reviews. Drawing these connections can help them see that science builds on the same reasoning skills they already use, but applies them with stricter rules and greater care.

Learning to evaluate the evidence on which claims are based can also offer us some protection from misinformation and fake news. We all encounter claims such as "The Earth is flat"; "Images of the moon landings were faked"; "Dinosaurs never existed – it's all a hoax." While these and similar claims may appear to be supported by evidence, that evidence often doesn't meet the criteria of reliability, validity, corroboration, coherence, and peer scrutiny. Here are some common warning signs:

- **Anecdotes instead of data**. "I heard about one person who…." Personal stories can be interesting, but they don't prove what's generally true.
- **Uncorroborated claims**. "There's a secret document that shows…." If no one else can check it, it isn't reliable evidence.
- **Cherry-picking**. Choosing one piece of data that fits a story while ignoring the bigger picture (e.g. "It snowed today, so global warming isn't real").
- **Appeals to the wrong authority**. "This famous person says…" An opinion from someone without relevant expertise carries little weight.
- **Stories instead of evidence**. A narrative that explains things away without providing any actual data (e.g. "All fossils were planted to trick us").
- **Lack of coherence**. A claim that requires us to believe something far less plausible than the mainstream explanation (e.g. a global conspiracy involving thousands of scientists).

Contrasting these weak forms of evidence with scientific practice – where data are public, testable, and open to challenge – we can begin to see why science offers a more trustworthy way of understanding the world.

In this lesson, pupils will evaluate evidence used to support the theory that an asteroid impact caused the mass extinction of dinosaurs 66 million years ago. They'll see that corroborating evidence has accumulated over the years, and that the theory is widely supported by the scientific community. Despite this, debate continues: there is evidence to suggest that volcanic activity played a significant role in the extinction. Scientific hypotheses and theories are always open to scrutiny and challenge, and as new evidence comes to light, those theories may change.

The lesson should help pupils to grasp that science does not ask us to believe blindly, but to weigh evidence carefully. It also shows them that science's strength lies not in certainty, but in its openness to new evidence and its willingness to correct itself over time.

Questions for reflection

- Can you recall a time when you observed something (gathered some data) that you used as evidence to support a possible explanation of events? How did you use "Maybe…" thinking to come up with a strong hypothesis from that evidence?
- How often do you pause to evaluate a piece of evidence before committing to a hypothesis? Could you make greater use of criteria such as reliability, validity, corroboration, coherence, and peer scrutiny?
- Think back to a time when you were persuaded by false claims. Did the source present "evidence" to make the claims seem true? Did this "evidence" have any of the warning signs listed earlier?
- As you teach some topics, could you place more emphasis on the evidence used to support scientific claims? Could it be useful to evaluate some of the evidence Darwin used to develop his theory of evolution? How was the primary evidence gathered by Mary Anning used to inform the

development of ideas about the history of life on Earth? How did Galileo use new empirical evidence to challenge accepted theories?

- How do you help pupils understand that scientific theories are not absolute truths but are based on evidence that can be challenged or refined over time?
- The scientific community corrects itself through peer review. Under what conditions could groups of pupils become self-correcting in a comparable way?
- In your view, could science teaching that emphasises the role of evidence help to protect children from misinformation and fake news?

Lesson 8

Notes for the busy teacher

Learning aim: I can evaluate evidence and list some of the reasons for trusting science

Young people (in fact, people generally) often struggle to know what or who to believe in a world full of misinformation. This lesson digs deeper into the idea of evidence and trust in science and the scientific community. Scientists gather empirical evidence, often to test a hypothesis. When enough supporting evidence has been gathered, the hypothesis becomes accepted – at least until some contradictory evidence is found. Crucially, the evidence is peer reviewed and tested by other scientists before being accepted; while individual scientists may be wrong, or even rogue, over time the scientific community corrects itself. This lesson engages pupils in evaluating some of the evidence that supports "the Alvarez hypothesis" – the idea that the extinction of the dinosaurs was caused by the collision of a large asteroid with the Earth 66 million years ago. In this case, the evidence is historical in nature. Pupils are asked to consider the features of good evidence, and to think about why science, or the scientific community, might be trusted.

Session plan

Skills building exercise (warm-up)

Remind the pupils of their rules and of the skills they have practised. Another important skill, or rather a disposition, is being open to changing one's mind in the face of a stronger argument or fresh evidence.

- Tell the class that you are going to share one or more contestable statements. They will need to move to indicate whether they agree or disagree with the statement. They will also need to share reasons for their decision.
- Assign one side of the classroom as "agree" and one side as "disagree." (In a variation of the exercise, you could assign the four corners of the room as "strongly agree," "weakly agree," "weakly disagree," and "strongly disagree.")
- Share a contestable statement (e.g. cats are better than dogs, ice-cream is better than cake, art is more

important than science, etc.). Give the pupils a little time to think, then ask them to move.

- Give each group some time to share their reasons. Can they combine their reasons to make a persuasive argument?
- Before the next step, remind pupils of the debate they had in Lesson 1. In a debate, it's easy to stop listening to the other side and to become overly committed to your own side; the object is to win. In this situation, the pupils should try to keep an open mind. They should listen carefully to the reasons and arguments they hear. The object is to achieve a richer understanding and make a more informed choice.
- Now allow each group to share their argument with the whole class (each group could choose a spokesperson, or a series of individuals could speak) while the others listen.
- You could allow some time for questions and counter-arguments.
- Now ask if anyone would like to change their mind – to physically "cross the floor."
- If people do switch, ask them to reflect on why they changed their mind. What did they hear that they hadn't thought of before? Have they now "lost the argument," or have they learned something new?
- Can the pupils think of a belief they used to hold, but no longer do? What caused them to change their minds?
- Reflect on the value of open-mindedness and of a willingness to change one's view (to be reasoned with). Also, reflect on the value of maintaining one's original position after having listened with care to all of the arguments. In both cases, a more informed choice has been made.

Stimulus and discussion

- Read Dinosaurs to the class.
- Discuss the story with the children, making use of the discussion plan provided as appropriate. Do the pupils have questions in response to the story? These could be addressed now or collected and addressed following the main activity.

Main exercise

- Tell the class that they are going to explore questions of good evidence and trust in scientists a little further by looking at what scientists say about why the dinosaurs became extinct around 66 million years ago.
- To orient the class, you could show an animation of the asteroid strike (this BBC video could be played from 2:10 onwards https://www.youtube.com/watch?v=DGu6ZPyKyJ0).
- Introduce Slide 7. This shows nine possible reasons for believing that the extinction of the dinosaurs was caused by a large asteroid hitting the Earth.
- Divide the class into groups of three. Their task is to think together to rank the reasons from most convincing to least convincing. They could use a diamond nine grid like the one shown on Slide 8 to do this (or they could place them on a continuum from most convincing to least convincing). The boxes are numbered so that pupils can simply write the numbers in the order of their choice. Alternatively, the exercise could be made into a card-sort which may support sustained thinking together.

- Remind the pupils to follow their ground rules and to practise being open to changing their view in the face of a better argument.
- As they finish, ask the groups to think together about why some of the reasons are more convincing than others.
- Review the groups' answers in plenary. Which reasons have the majority of groups identified as convincing? Why so? Here are some thoughts that might be teased out:
  - The Chicxulub crater and the iridium layer are strong pieces of primary physical (empirical) evidence. Both date to around the time of the dinosaur extinction, and both are strongly suggestive of a sufficiently large asteroid impact; they both fit well with the Alvarez hypothesis.
  - Peer review (scientists giving the wider scientific community the chance to take a critical look at their work) is a crucial part of the way science works. It can help to spot mistakes, and the reviewers are less likely to be biased than the original scientists, who are often very invested in their work. This gives us a reason to trust scientific evidence.
  - The fact that a Nobel Prize-winning scientist was persuaded by the evidence in favour of an asteroid impact is certainly more convincing than the opinion of a lay person (Jack the butcher!). However, the opinion of one scientist, no matter how distinguished, is less convincing than the opinion of the scientific community that has been formed over time.

- The presence of craters on the moon suggests that asteroids have also collided with Earth (though it doesn't show that a large asteroid hit at the time of the extinction), and the fact that the dinosaurs disappeared from the fossil record over a short time period suggests some sort of sudden change (while this could have been caused by an asteroid there are other explanations). These are also useful pieces of physical evidence, though perhaps they are less convincing.
- While computer-generated animations can be a useful way of visualising an event such as an asteroid impact, they are, at best, based on physical evidence – they do not themselves constitute evidence (more sophisticated modelling techniques should be treated differently).
- The fact that some scientists oppose the asteroid hypothesis and favour an alternative explanation is obviously not a convincing reason to believe in it! This leads into the whole-class plenary.

Whole-class plenary

- Show the final slide.
- How do the pupils respond to Karl, Grace, and Molly-with-a-y?
- What could Tala mean when she says, "Maybe that's why we can trust science"? An idea to tease out might be that the scientific community bases its beliefs on evidence. As a whole, the community is open to changing its view if new evidence comes to light. It isn't tied to one belief and doesn't change the evidence

to sustain that belief (though individual scientists might be tempted to do this!). The scientific community is **self-correcting**.

Metacognition

Give the groups of three time to think together about the following questions:

- Did the pupils manage to remain open-minded today? Were there examples of them yielding to stronger arguments or maintaining their view after listening carefully to challenges?
- Why is it important to be open to changing your view – to being reasoned with?
- Can groups of ordinary people be self-correcting, like the scientific community?
- Which other rules did the groups do well with? Why were they useful?
- Are there rules they need to focus on more next time? How will they help?

Resources

- Slide set to support the session
- Hard copies of Slides 7 and 8 may be useful to support group work. You might prefer to turn the exercise into a card-sort as this is likely to further support sustained thinking together.

Talk prompts and vocabulary

Talk prompts

For this lesson's thinking together and working scientifically foci: "I agree with… because…"; "I disagree with... because…"; "The strongest reason I have heard is…"; "I'm sticking with my original choice because…"; "I have changed my mind because…."

Vocabulary

Evaluate: in this context, to decide what is more valuable, persuasive, or important.

Evidence: facts or information that are used to decide whether a belief or claim is true.

Peer review: evaluation of scientific, academic, or professional work by others working in the same field **or, for children**, scientists evaluating each other's work).

Open-mindedness: a disposition of being open to other views and the possibility of changing one's view; being open to reason and being reasoned with.

The scientific community: a diverse, worldwide network of scientists who interact with each other, sharing their research and checking each other's work.

Self-correction: acknowledging and correcting one's own errors.

Stimulus: Dinosaurs

Mr Robins had been standing there for a good two or three minutes. Everyone else had gradually noticed and fallen silent. But Karl and Molly-with-a-y were completely absorbed in their own conversation. "No, they never really existed. I watched a video on YouTube and they said it was all made up," Karl protested.

Molly looked like she was ready to bang her head on the desk. "Two things. One: dinosaurs did exist – I've seen them in the museum. Two: just because you watched a video on YouTube doesn't mean that it's true."

Mr Robins looked faintly amused but cleared his throat loudly so that Karl and Molly finally looked away from each other.

"All right", he said, "let me get this right. Karl, you saw a video on YouTube that convinced you that dinosaurs aren't real. Molly, you disagree." They both nodded.

"It's like Ama's wonky sheep all over again!" muttered Molly.

"No, it's not!" exclaimed Karl. "I've seen evidence!"

"Not good evidence," Molly retorted.

"Well, what is good evidence then?" shot back Karl.

"That, Karl, is an excellent question," said Mr Robins.

"Well, people have been digging up dinosaur fossils for years, for starters! People you can trust, too, like those dinosaur scientists – palaeo-whatdyecallums...."

"Palaeontologists?" offered Mr Robins.

"Yes – them. Not silly YouTubers! Anyone can make a YouTube video." Molly was getting exasperated.

"Yes – but the video said that palaeontologists have been fooled. You see, lots of the fossils they found are clever fakes put there a couple of hundred years ago by people who wanted to make us believe in dragons and monsters and suchlike – that's why people didn't find fossils before then."

"But that's not evidence, Karl, it's just a story!" Molly exclaimed.

Undeterred, Karl went on, "Besides, there would still be some dinosaurs around if there had once been so many of them. Nobody has ever seen an actual dinosaur."

"So you can only believe something if you have seen it with your own eyes?" Molly asked, incredulously. "Do you believe in Mount Everest, Karl, or that Henry the Eighth was real?"

"I suppose so," Karl replied.

"There you go then. Sometimes we just have to trust the evidence." Molly said.

"Yes, but that still leaves us asking what kind of evidence we should trust," said Mr Robins, thoughtfully. "And who we can trust. "Can you really trust a scientist more than a YouTuber?"

Discussion plan

- Do you think that you can only really believe something if you have seen it for yourself?
- Imagine you never believed anything you hadn't seen for yourself. What would be good about this? What would be bad?
- Is there a difference between believing something is true and knowing it is true? Can you give an example of each?
- Imagine someone told you that aliens lived on the moon. What evidence would you need before you believed them?
- What do you think makes good evidence?
- What would make you change your mind about something you believed before?

- Do you think we can believe palaeontologists (scientists who study fossils) more than we can believe YouTubers? Why or why not?
- Do you believe that dinosaurs really lived on the Earth? What evidence do you have?
- Most scientists – let's call them "the scientific community" – believe that dinosaurs lived on the Earth between 245 and 66 million years ago. Does that help to convince you that they were real? Why or why not?

9

Looking back, looking forward

Looking at the science

Throughout this book, we've explored science as a set of ways of thinking that helps us make sense of the world. We've paid particular attention to three forms of reasoning: "Maybe..." thinking, where possible explanations are suggested; "If... then..." thinking, where those explanations are tested; and "So the rule is..." thinking, where patterns are noticed and tentative generalisations are formed. These ways of thinking have been introduced through activities and lessons intended to be enjoyable and meaningful for children. In this final chapter, we step back to consider how these ideas could frame your science teaching more generally.

DOI: 10.4324/9781003663454-10

Looking back, one feature of the TTiPS lessons is that they don't depend on elaborate equipment or require you to follow scripts. Instead, they rely on curiosity, dialogue, and a willingness to treat children's ideas as resources for learning. This draws on a view of science as an ongoing, unending dialogue that leads to better questions rather than to final answers. The aim of these activities is to teach children to think more like scientists by drawing them into the big dialogue of science. Looking forward, could this suggest a different way of approaching curriculum topics?

Your planning may already begin with both knowledge-based objectives and objectives based on what it means to work scientifically. The latter are most likely focused on teaching practical skills. Could you now ask yourself how a topic could be framed as a sequence of experiences that invite children into the distinctive forms of thinking that science values?

The following sequence of activities illustrates how abductive, deductive, and inductive reasoning can provide a loose but purposeful structure for inquiry – one that leaves room for uncertainty, scepticism, and further questions to emerge. Purposefully, this is not a lesson plan; it's more of a signpost, hinting at one possible way of adapting your practice.

We'll take as our example a topic on materials and their properties that includes an exploration of dissolving. Such a topic features in Year 5 of the English National Curriculum. The activities show how a single phenomenon – what happens when solids like sugar or salt are mixed with water – can give children repeated opportunities to suggest explanations, test them, and notice patterns. It also illustrates how curiosity, dialogue, and careful attention to evidence can guide both thinking and learning.

Stimulus

It can be stimulating to begin with a puzzle. You could demonstrate – or allow pupils to find out – what happens when a teaspoon of salt or sugar is added to cold water and stirred. You could also weigh a cup of water, dissolve some sugar in it, and ask the pupils to predict whether the weight will have increased, decreased, or remained the same.

Pupils might raise questions: where does the salt go? Does it disappear? Is it still there? Why does it get heavier? Hopefully, their curiosity is aroused, and they are invested in the learning.

"Maybe..." thinking (abduction and hypothesis formation)

Now you can remind the children about "Maybe..." thinking. Can they think together to suggest what might be going on?

They could make hypotheses such as: maybe sugar and salt dissolve because the water breaks them up into tiny bits that you can't see. Maybe the sugar is hiding between the water bits. Maybe it spreads out all through the water instead of staying in one place. Maybe it gets heavier because some of the sugar disappears but a bit stays and we can't see that little bit. Maybe the salt has melted.

The children are using limited evidence as a foundation for creating possible explanations that are consistent with their current understanding of materials. You have the option to facilitate some whole-class dialogue around the hypotheses – which seem more likely and why?

"If... then..." thinking (deduction and prediction)

You could ask the children to focus on one of the hypotheses, or each group could work with their own. Can they think together to test their idea using "If... then..." thinking?

Suggestions might include: if the solid is broken into tiny bits that stay in the water, then the water should weigh more after the solid has dissolved. If all the sugar is still there, then the mixture should weigh the same as the water and sugar added together. If dissolving happens because water breaks the solid into tiny pieces, then stirring should make it dissolve faster. If breaking up is the key, then larger pieces should take longer to dissolve than smaller ones. If the solid is still present in tiny bits, then letting the water evaporate should leave the solid behind again.

The children can now gather empirical evidence – observations and simple measurements – to test their ideas. There may be an opportunity to think together about what the evidence means: does it support the children's hypotheses, or does it not? How do they feel about this? An attitude of scepticism might come into play: "Hang on a minute… was that really a fair test? What might have affected the result?"

"So the rule is…" thinking (induction and generalisation)

The children may have concluded that sugar and salt really are broken into tiny pieces by water and that this is called dissolving. You could remind them of their learning about "So the rule is…" thinking: can they think together to suggest rules about dissolving? How much evidence do they have to support their rule? How much more would they need before they had confidence in their rule? How could they go about gathering this evidence?

Suggested rules might include: so the rule is… water breaks solids up into small pieces that you can't see (it dissolves them); water dissolves white substances with crystals; whenever a solid dissolves in water, the mixture weighs the same as the solid and the water before they were mixed.

Hopefully, the children will acknowledge that their "rules" are tentative because they are based on limited evidence (they are rules "for now"). Their suggestions can be used as a starting point for further inquiry. They could go on to experiment with solids such as citric acid, bicarbonate of soda, or instant coffee granules. These might lead them to refine their hypotheses: bicarbonate of soda may leave the water slightly cloudy – does this mean it's partially soluble? Coffee granules are not white – does colour really matter?

Solids such as flour, rice, sand, or cornflour will cause further cognitive conflict. And then there are questions about whether liquids and gases dissolve too, or whether water is the only solvent. In other words, our inquiry isn't ended here – we're drawn back to the formation of fresh questions and fresh hypotheses that lead us into a deepening and unending dialogue about the nature of the world around us.

Two notes of caution. First, as we noted in the introduction, teaching effectively through dialogue relies on good subject knowledge. You'll find the framework of generic "talk moves" helpful in making the switch from an authoritative to a dialogic mode of communication, but you'll need to combine them with secure subject knowledge to truly develop children's thinking.

Second, remember that we're not advocating that you teach in a dialogic mode all the time. Authoritative communication – careful explanation, modelling, and demonstration – is essential. The key is to develop your professional judgement about when to switch from one mode to the other.

Looking at your learning

We very much hope that you – and the children you teach – have enjoyed the TTiPS experience. It's an approach based on a dialogic view of education. In this view, we should – some of the time – teach **through** dialogue so that learning is more meaningful and deeper. We should also teach **for** dialogue, so that children get better at thinking together and are equipped to join dialogues in the various communities they may become part of – including the scientific community. Learning, we believe, should proceed through the inter-animation of different voices or perspectives – including those of the children.

This means that learners of any age should be viewed not as passive recipients of new knowledge, but as partners in the co-construction of new knowledge. In that spirit, we'd like to invite you to engage in some final reflection on your own learning.

Following is a list of statements. They are **contestable**: they reflect our beliefs but may not fully align with your own. For each statement, consider the extent of your agreement or disagreement. Hopefully, this will help you to crystallise your own – always provisional – conclusions.

1. **The TTiPS approach will help children to identify more strongly with science – to see it as a subject that could be for them.**
   If yes, how could you adapt your teaching to maximise the impact? If no, what alternative approaches might encourage this sense of identity?
2. **Children's curiosity should guide the questions we explore in science, rather than curriculum objectives alone.**
   What examples from your teaching might support or challenge this approach?
3. **Children's initial explanations are not obstacles to learning science but essential starting points for it.**
   How do you typically respond when pupils' ideas differ from accepted scientific explanations?

4 **Science learning can and should help children connect everyday experiences with disciplinary knowledge.**
How could you help pupils notice the similarities and differences between their everyday ways of explaining the world and scientific approaches?

5 **Abductive, deductive, and inductive reasoning, with a healthy dose of scepticism, provide a practical framework for structuring inquiry.**
Can you think of sequences of lessons where this would or would not work well?

6 **Scientific knowledge should be presented to children as reliable but always open to revision.**
Can young children hold these two ideas at the same time?

7 **The strength of good group work lies in the way pupils think together. In this respect, it mirrors science itself: the strength of science lies in the way the scientific community thinks together.**
In what ways is this comparison helpful? Where might it break down?

8 **Learning to engage in dialogue is an important foundation for thinking scientifically.**
In what ways does classroom dialogue resemble – or differ from – the ways scientists test ideas, challenge explanations, and build knowledge together?

9 **The TTiPS approach will make children better prepared for encounters with misinformation or "fake news."**
Can reasoning skills learned in science really transfer to other areas of life?

10 **Thinking together supports learning across the curriculum, not just in science.**

Is it feasible or even desirable to create opportunities for thinking together while maintaining a focus on subject-specific learning goals?

11 **Teaching through and for dialogue is not so much a technique as it is an attitude towards pupils' thinking and the co-construction of knowledge**.
What are the implications of your answer for the way you teach?

A final question for you: looking back over these reflections, what is the single most important insight or question that you will carry into your teaching?

Looking further afield

Well, that's the end of the book, but hopefully not the end of your engagement with TTiPS, or with Thinking Together. We'd be delighted to have your reflections on the book and its impact on your class – do reach out to us and help us to refine the approach.

Before we go, perhaps we can share one more contestable statement that would be our main take-away:

> Teaching through and for dialogue is the most important component of any approach to oracy.

Look around you. Look in the classroom, look at the wider community, your nation, and the world. Would these places be better if the next generation were able to reason together across their differences, attend carefully to evidence, and include each other's perspectives in a shared story about what it might mean to live well together? We think they would. What do you think?

Appendix 1
Supporting effective group work

Ground rules

As noted in the introduction, effective collaborative group work is far more likely if children are taught how to do it. The creation and consistent use of a set of ground rules is a tried and tested method for teaching children to think together in a group. Chapter 2 includes detailed guidance on this.

Your ground rules will support effective group work across the curriculum, especially if you make active use of them. Having the ground rules in front of the pupils during group work will support their use.

You might consider choosing a focus ground rule each week and spending a short time teaching pupils how to follow it. Rules such as "We challenge each other's ideas respectfully" need to be unpicked. What different kinds of challenge are there? What does it mean to offer counterexamples or spot assumptions? What language can I use in order to challenge respectfully? Sharing relevant talk prompts of the kind shown in this appendix and giving pupils opportunities to practise using them, perhaps in the context of games such as those used in the TTiPS warm-up activities, could be useful.

At the end of lessons or days and at the end of the week, you could reflect together on the impact the focus ground rule has had and decide whether to move on to a new rule. Over time, pupils will become more metacognitively aware of the value of the ground rules and the language they can use to follow them. They might internalise the rules and apply them in a range of different contexts, which could have a significantly positive impact on their learning and on their wider lives.

Group size

Pupils are often asked to work in pairs and are sometimes assigned a "talk-partner" in their class. Opportunities for talk in pairs can be very valuable: well-known structures like "think-pair-share" work well. Talk in pairs is quick to organise, it usually feels safe for the pupils, and it gives them valuable opportunities to rehearse their ideas and hear the ideas of others.

In pairs, only two perspectives are available, and this can be a disadvantage for more complex tasks. Pairs can be prone to reach agreement quickly, perhaps because of the absence of another point of view. Sometimes, this means that useful challenges are not made and valuable alternatives go unconsidered.

Groups of three can work very well, and this is the group size that tends to be recommended in the TTiPS lesson plans. The third voice can offer necessary challenge and help bring alternatives to light. This can create a degree of cognitive conflict and encourage the group to "think harder" as they reason their way towards a resolution.

In their original research on Thinking Together, Neil Mercer, Lyn Dawes, and Rupert Wegerif also noticed that, when collaborating in a three, members of a group are likely to have short periods during which they are not talking – they get a chance to reflect. These moments of reflection can give rise to insights that help to move the pupils' shared thinking forward.

Larger groups offer more perspectives, but these can be difficult to manage, making reasoning and resolution challenging. Larger groups also have a tendency to fragment – a group of six soon becomes two threes or three twos as pupils are impatient to share their views. If you do need to ask pupils to work in larger groups, some of the following approaches to structuring group work might be useful.

As far as the composition of the groups is concerned, you know your pupils best. Mixed ability groupings can be helpful (see Appendix 2 on Inclusion), but you will have your own views on this. It's worth noting that grouping a quieter child with one more confident can lead to the quieter child being dominated even in a small group discussion. Many pupils report liking the opportunity to work with different people over time, so we would recommend varying the groups.

Structuring group work

Here are some simple ideas that might be particularly useful for larger groups.

Use a "talking stick." It doesn't have to be a stick! The idea is that one pupil holds an object that singles them out as the speaker – everyone else is listening. Only when the speaker chooses to pass the object on – which should be after a relatively short contribution – may someone else speak. This is a scaffold that can be withdrawn, but may just help to get the pupils into the habit of speaking one at a time and listening carefully to each other.

Assign talk roles. If everyone in the group has a particular job to do, they're more likely to stay engaged. Roles might include noting down the more significant things that have been said to reduce strain on working memory, initiating a line of inquiry, summarising what's been said, building on others' ideas, offering challenge, and so on. The UK charity Voice 21 refers to this approach as "Talk Tactics," and have role cards including relevant sentence stems on their website.[1]

Pupils should take different roles over time and should become more metacognitively aware of the value of the role and how to perform it. Ideally, you would be able to reduce their dependency on the cards over time so that any pupil can perform any role during a group discussion.

Use talk tokens. A common failing of group work is that not all voices are heard. This can be because some pupils are naturally quiet, or because others are prone to talk too much! Giving each pupil a fixed number of opportunities to contribute – represented by tokens – can be a way of enabling everyone to be heard.

Quiet pupils are encouraged to use at least one of their tokens, while more confident pupils are limited, typically to three turns. Having a limited number of turns can encourage pupils to evaluate what they want to share so that they don't waste turns with trivial contributions.

Topsy Page has written about these and numerous other strategies to support group work in her recent book, *100 Ideas for Primary Teachers: Oracy*.[2]

Classroom layout

The world over, groups convening for dialogue sit in a circle. There are three primary reasons for this. First, it allows everyone to see each other and to show attentive listening. Second, it positions everyone with equal status – no one has more power than anyone else. Third, a circle doesn't have sides – pupils are not positioned in a way that could encourage an adversarial approach. All these things are important for effective thinking together.

Where possible, then, groups should be arranged in a shape as close to a circle as the space allows – for groups of three, each pupil can occupy one corner of a triangle.

When the whole class is engaged in an extended episode of thinking together, they should ideally be seated in a circle. Although this can be challenging in some classrooms, you'll be rewarded with a noticeably better quality of communication founded on careful listening. The teacher should be part of the circle; this is important because it signals the switch from the authoritative style of communication described in the introduction to the facilitative style. It's a visual reminder to all involved that the "game" is changing – the pupils' role is no longer to provide the teacher with correct answers, but to think together with their classmates.

Pupil talk prompts

In the introduction, we suggested that the teacher as facilitator should encourage pupils to: be heard and understood; listen to each other; think harder; think together. We shared examples of questions you can use to call for these behaviours. Confident facilitation by you will provide them with a model of thinking together that they can internalise and apply, even when collaborating in small groups without your facilitation.

Another useful way of supporting pupils to develop the desired behaviours is to share talk prompts like those shown next. Sharing too many talk prompts at one time could be confusing, so consider carefully selecting the prompts that align with the behaviours and ground rules you are focusing on.

In the introduction, we suggested that it could be useful to focus on the behaviours in the order in which they are listed ("Making yourself heard and understood" first), so that pupils build their skills progressively, though this isn't a necessity. It should be noted that each TTiPS lesson has a focus skill, and some suggested language related to that skill is included in each lesson plan.

Making yourself heard and understood

- "I think…"
- "In my opinion…"

- "My idea is..."
- "Maybe..."
- "I wonder if..."
- "Is it possible that...?"
- "An example of that is..."
- "What I'm trying to say is..."

Showing that you're listening to others

- "So you're saying that..."
- "I heard you say that..."
- "Do you mean that...?"
- "Let me check I've understood you..."
- "One important thing you said is..."
- "I hadn't thought about... until you said..."
- "I'd like to thank A for saying..."
- "I learned something new from..."
- "Can you say more about...?"
- "I have a question for A...";
- "The thing that stood out for me is..."
- "My main take-aways are..."
- "So, to summarise..."

Thinking harder

- "I think... because..."
- "One reason for this could be..."
- "This could be explained by..."
- "The evidence shows..."
- "The evidence for that is..."
- "Another possibility is..."
- "Another perspective on this is..."
- "That would mean that..."

- "If… then…"
- "I'm not convinced yet because…"
- "We're still unsure about…"
- "We could check this by…"
- "A counter example is…"
- "We're assuming that…"
- "These things are alike / the same because…"
- "These things are different because…"
- "A pattern I notice is…"
- "So the rule is…"
- "So in general…"

Thinking together

- "I agree / disagree with A because…"
- "I see it differently because…"
- "Does anyone have a different view?"
- "Responding to A…"
- "Building on what A said…"
- "An extra point to add to A's idea is…"
- "This links with what A said because…"
- "What do others think about A's idea?"
- "What do you think, A?"
- "So, are we agreeing that…?"

Notes

1 Voice 21. "Classroom Practice Toolkit: Student Talk Tactics," Voice 21, 2022, PDF file, accessed February 26, 2026, https://voice21.org/wp-content/uploads/2022/09/Voice21-ClassroomPracticeToolkit-StudentTalkTactics.pdf

2 Topsy Page. *100 Ideas for Primary Teachers: Oracy*. (Bloomsbury Education, 2024).

Appendix 2
Tips for including pupils with Special Educational Needs and Disabilities (SEND) by Wendy Lee of Lingo

Science is such an exciting subject for pupils to engage with. A few adaptations for pupils with SEND can ensure they understand the topic more readily and take part in the rich discussions that support deeper learning.

For some pupils, the language of science can be challenging – it is a topic with lots of new and long words that can feel overwhelming, though we can support pupils by explaining and breaking down key words that will ultimately not only support their engagement in science but support those crucial word-learning skills.

The joy of science for SEND pupils is that it can be practical and visual, which allows for different ways to access learning other than through language alone.

A few simple classroom adaptations can help pupils with SEND access science and develop their oracy skills:

Check understanding by asking children to explain the task in their own words, breaking it into manageable parts, and giving extra processing time.

- Children with SEND often take more time to both process and formulate responses.
- Be explicit about giving more time – "I'm just going to give you some thinking time."
- Support pupils to seek clarification when they struggle to understand.
- Create a climate and safe space where asking questions is seen as a positive – an opportunity for learning for all.

Adapt adult language based on what you know about the children's levels of language so that they can get the best out of oracy teaching and learning, for example:

- Give instructions in "chunks" so they can follow what they need to do.
- Use bullet pointed lists – first do x then y.
- Give choices – e.g. tell me what you like best about science… is it testing out your ideas or planning your experiments?
- Think about question levels for pupils with SEND – questions relating to concrete experiences are much easier than more abstract questions outside the "here and now". Also "what" questions are much easier than how or why questions.
- Use commentary to support engagement – "I like the look of your kite," or "tell me about your kite" rather than "how did you decide what kind of tail to add to your kite?"

Use visual aids to help with understanding and engagement, for example:

- Use pictures to show key ideas, such as a picture of a kite with a tail in Chapter 3.
- Provide visual aids for equipment needed so pupils know what to expect.
- When using sentence stems, provide a visual symbol if needed – a simple pile of bricks, for example, to represent building on an idea. Or use gestures to represent different aspects of discussion, such as add, build, and challenge.
- Use emoticons to help understanding of emotions when talking about how they feel about discussions or learning.
- Visual checklists can be helpful to reflect on learning or check all tasks have been completed or equipment gathered.

Teach key vocabulary explicitly as this can make a huge difference to understanding a task or concept.

- Check out some of the explanations we give for scientific words to make sure children understand. For example, explaining **intuitive** as being based on instinct and **rational** being based on reason. We might need to give specific examples and ensure children understand these key terms.
- Build reinforcement of this key vocabulary into practical learning tasks to help make them stick.
- It's also useful to teach words used in science that are not specific to the topic – Tier 2 words, such as intuition, predict, or summarise can be worth a bit of time to ensure pupils understand.

Classroom dialogue

- During group work, try putting mixed ability groups together. It supports the more confident children to explain things in detail and practise taking conversational turns, and also helps those pupils with lower levels of language to hear and take part in rich discussions.

- Give students specific roles or tasks in group work that can help them to engage and not feel overwhelmed in busy group discussions.
- Give guidance or models to support discussions for pupils with SEND – make it explicit so pupils hear and are given labels for the type of talk happening, for example, "I loved your reasoning there, you worked out that if you tested the different ways of making a tail for your kite, it had more chance of success."
- Adaptations to questions can be helpful to encourage engagement, for example in the plane experiment in Chapter 3, children are asked to make comparisons between planes – it might be useful to give some options for SEND pupils to guide them – e.g. what do you think about the size, shape, symmetry, strength etc.?
- Some pupils may struggle to read facial expressions or body language so it is useful to provide explicit feedback to these pupils to help them join in and receive feedback on their contributions.

We're very grateful to Wendy Lee for these notes. Wendy has over 35 years of experience working with children across all educational settings. Her diverse background includes roles as a therapist, lecturer, and professional director for The Communication Trust. Wendy has contributed to national campaigns, developed interventions like Talk Boost, and created resources for practitioners. She is currently Professional Director at Lingo (https://www.lingospeech.co.uk/).

Index

INDEX

INDEX

For Product Safety Concerns and Information please contact our EU representative GPSR@taylorandfrancis.com
Taylor & Francis Verlag GmbH, Kaufingerstraße 24, 80331 München, Germany

www.ingramcontent.com/pod-product-compliance
Lightning Source LLC
LaVergne TN
LVHW022001280826
846781LV00023B/232

* 9 7 8 1 0 4 1 1 2 1 7 3 2 *